Workshop on Meaning Relations Between Phases and Sentences (RELATIONS 2019)

AA001507

Gothenburg, Sweden
23 May 2019

ISBN: 978-1-5108-8764-0

Printed from e-media with permission by:

Curran Associates, Inc.
57 Morehouse Lane
Red Hook, NY 12571

CURRAN ASSOCIATES INC. proceedings.com

Some format issues inherent in the e-media version may also appear in this print version.

Copyright© (2019) by the Association for Computational Linguistics
All rights reserved.

Printed by Curran Associates, Inc. (2019)

For permission requests, please contact the Association for Computational Linguistics
at the address below.

Association for Computational Linguistics
209 N. Eighth Street
Stroudsburg, Pennsylvania 18360

Phone: 1-570-476-8006
Fax: 1-570-476-0860

acl@aclweb.org

Additional copies of this publication are available from:

Curran Associates, Inc.
57 Morehouse Lane
Red Hook, NY 12571 USA
Phone: 845-758-0400
Fax: 845-758-2633
Email: curran@proceedings.com
Web: www.proceedings.com

RELATIONS 2019

RELATIONS - Workshop on meaning relations between phrases and sentences

May 23, 2019

Gothenburg, Sweden

This workshop was organized by:

©2019 The Association for Computational Linguistics

Introduction

This workshop brings together researchers working on comparing the meaning of linguistic expressions such as phrases, clauses, sentences, and paragraphs. Comparisons of multiple expressions identify meaning relations such as paraphrase, textual entailment, contradiction, specificity, and semantic similarity.

We want to promote the collaboration between researchers working on the different tasks, and to encourage reusability of ideas, resources, and systems. We offer a venue for different researchers to share their work and to discuss the implications on and the interactions with other related areas and tasks.

We are interested in both: theoretical research on the nature of meaning relations and the empirical work on identifying, generating, and extracting them. We also invited submissions studying the impact of the relations in downstream applications.

The first edition of the workshop is collocated with the IWCS 2019 conference in Gothenburg, Sweden, where all accepted papers will be presented orally.

We would like to thank the authors, the reviewers and attendees for making the first edition of this workshop a successful endeavor.

Venelin Kovatchev
Darina Gold
Torsten Zesch

Organizers

Venelin Kovatchev, Language and Computation Center, University of Barcelona
Darina Gold (née Benikova), Language Technology Lab, University of Duisburg-Essen
Torsten Zesch, Language Technology Lab, University of Duisburg-Essen

Program Committee:

Ahmed Abúraed, Universitat Pompeu Fabra
Chris Biemann, Universität Hamburg
Sam Bowman, New York University
Philipp Cimiano, University of Bielefeld
Ido Dagan, Bar-Ilan University
Thierry Declerck, Saarland University
Mona Diab, George Washington University
Anette Frank, University of Heidelberg
Amir Hazem, Université de Nantes
Andrea Horbach, University of Duisburg-Essen
Tobias Horsmann, University of Duisburg-Essen
Omer Levy, University of Washington
M. Antonia Martí, Universitat de Barcelona
Nafise Moosavi, Technische Universität Darmstadt
Simon Ostermann, Saarland University
Sebastian Pado, Universität Stuttgart
Michael Roth, University of Stuttgart
Peter Schüller, Technische Universität Wien
Vered Shvartz, Bar-Ilan University
Sanja Stajner, Symanto Research GmbH
Irina Temnikova, Sofia University
Michael Wojatzki, University of Duisburg-Essen
Marcos Zampieri, University of Wolverhampton

This page intentionally left blank.

Table of Contents

This page intentionally left blank.

Workshop Program

Thursday 23.05.2019

10:30 - 12:00 Session 1

10:30 - 11:00
Welcome to the RELATIONS workshop.

11:00 - 11:30
Maria Becker, Michael Staniek, Vivi Nastase and Anette Frank
Assessing the Difficulty of Classifying ConceptNet Relations in a Multi-Label Classification Setting

11:30 - 12:00
Nina Khairova, Svitlana Petrasova, Orken Mamyrbayev and Kuralay Mukhsina
Detecting Collocations Similarity via Logical-Linguistic Model

12:00 - 13:30 Lunch Break

13:30 - 15:30 Session 2

13:30 - 14:00
Frieda Josi, Christian Wartena and Ulrich Heid
Detecting Paraphrases of Standard Clause Titles in Insurance Contracts

14:00 - 14:30
Mark-Christoph Mueller
Semantic Matching of Documents from Heterogeneous Collections: A Simple and Transparent Method for Practical Applications

14:30 - 15:30
Discussion Panel.

15:30 - 16:00 Coffee Break

16:00 - 17:00 Invited talk by Gemma Boleda

17:00 - 17:30 Closing remarks

Assessing the Difficulty of Classifying ConceptNet Relations in a Multi-Label Classification Setting

Maria Becker, Michael Staniek, Vivi Nastase, and Anette Frank
Heidelberg University, Department of Computational Linguistics
{mbecker/staniek/nastase/frank}@cl.uni-heidelberg.de

Abstract

Commonsense knowledge relations are crucial for advanced NLU tasks. We examine the learnability of such relations as represented in CONCEPTNET, taking into account their *specific properties*, which can make relation classification difficult: a given concept pair can be linked by multiple relation types, and relations can have multi-word arguments of diverse semantic types. We explore a neural *open world multi-label classification approach* that focuses on the evaluation of classification accuracy for individual relations. Based on an in-depth study of the specific properties of the CONCEPTNET resource, we investigate the impact of different relation representations and model variations. Our analysis reveals that the complexity of argument types and relation ambiguity are the most important challenges to address. We design a customized evaluation method to address the incompleteness of the resource that can be expanded in future work.

1 Introduction

Commonsense knowledge can be seen as a large amount of diverse but simple facts about the world, people and everyday life, e.g., *Cars are used to travel* or *Birds can fly* (Liebermann, 2008). Commonsense knowledge obtained from CONCEPTNET is increasingly used in advanced NLU tasks, such as textual entailment (Weissenborn et al., 2018), reading comprehension (Mihaylov and Frank, 2018), machine comprehension (Wang and Li, 2018; José-Angel González and Hurtado Oliver, Lluís and Segarra, Encarna and Pla, Ferran, 2018), question answering (Ostermann et al., 2018) or dialogue modeling (Young et al., 2018) and also applications in vision (Le et al., 2013). Some of these approaches exploit embeddings learned from CONCEPTNET, others select specific relations from it, depending on the application.

This paper proposes a multi-label neural approach for classifying CONCEPTNET relations, where the task is to predict one (or several) commonsense relations from a given set of relation types that hold between two given concepts from CONCEPTNET. In future work, the predicted relations can then be used for enriching CONCEPTNET by adding relations between concepts which are not yet linked in the network.

We design the task of multi-label neural relational classification to account for specific properties of CONCEPTNET:

(i) CONCEPTNET's relation inventory is not designed to be disjunct: a given pair of relation arguments (in CONCEPTNET: *concepts*) may be connected by more than one relation type: e.g. ⟨*people*,DESIRES/CAPABLEOF,*eating in groups*⟩, ⟨*reading*,USEDFOR/CAUSES,*education*⟩. This places relations in close vicinity in semantic space, making relation prediction a hard task.

(ii) Concepts often are *multi-word expressions* of *different phrase types* (e.g., noun or verb phrases), posing a challenge for argument representation. Relation slots may also be filled by *different semantic types*: e.g., the 2nd argument of DESIRES can be an entity or event. Such heterogeneous signatures increase classification difficulty.

(iii) As any knowledge resource, CONCEPTNET is incomplete, which means that relations between concepts are missing. The incompleteness of the resource poses serious evaluation problems, since assumed negative instances may in fact be positive.

To tackle these issues we perform a thorough experimental examination of the learnability of CONCEPTNET relations in a controlled multi-label classification setting. Our contributions are: (i) a cleaned and balanced data subset covering the 14 most frequent relation types from the core part of CONCEPTNET that serves as a basis for assessing relation-specific classification performance. We extend this dataset to an open-world classification setup; (ii) a neural multi-label classification approach with various model options for the representation of relations and their (multi-word) arguments, including relation-specific label prediction thresholds; (iii) an in-depth analysis of specific properties of the CONCEPTNET relation inventory, from which we derive hypotheses that we evaluate in classification experiments; (iv) we perform detailed analysis of results that confirm a great number of our hypotheses regarding specific classification challenges; (v) finally, we assess the amount of potential evaluation discrepancies due to the incompleteness of the resource in a small-scale annotation experiment.

2 Related Work

2.1 Semantic Relation Classification

Semantic relation classification covers a wide range of methods and learning paradigms for representing relation instances (see Nastase et al. 2013 for an overview). Typically, the data is presented to the learner as independent instances, with or without a sentential context. Relation classification models represent the meaning of the arguments (attributional features) and if context is available, also the relation (relational features).

Recently Deep Learning has strongly influenced semantic relation learning. Word embeddings can provide attributional features for a variety of learning frameworks (Attia et al., 2016; Vylomova et al., 2016), and the sentential context – in its entirety, or only the structured (through grammatical relations) or unstructured phrase expressing the relation – can be modeled through a variety of neural architectures – CNN (Tan et al., 2018; Ren et al., 2018) or RNN variations (Zhang et al., 2018).

2.2 CONCEPTNET Relation Classification

Speer et al. (2008) introduce AnalogySpace, a representation of concepts and relations in CONCEPTNET built by factorizing a matrix with concepts on one axis and their features or properties (according to CONCEPTNET) on the other. This low-dimensional representation allows for finding analogous facts, generalizations, new categories and justifications for classifications based on known properties. While this representation allows for recomputing the confidence of existing facts, the focus was not on classifying or trying to learn specific relations represented in the resource.

Li et al. (2016) apply *matrix factorization* to CONCEPTNET with the aim of resource extension and report 91% accuracy in a *binary* evaluation (i.e., verifying the correctness of an (unlabeled) link between concepts). Saito et al. (2018) expand this work by combining the knowledge base completion task (distinguishing true relation triples consisting of arbitrary phrases from false ones) with the task of knowledge generation (finding the second entity for a given first entity and a given relation). They enhance the link prediction model of Li et al. with a model that learns the two tasks – knowledge base completion and knowledge generation – jointly and outperform the completion accuracy results of Li et al. by up to 3pp.

Many NLU tasks rely on *specific relations* from CONCEPTNET (Le et al., 2013; Shudo et al., 2016). It is thus important to assess classification accuracy for individual relation types.

3 The Difficulty of CONCEPTNET Relation Classification

3.1 CONCEPTNET Dataset

The Open Mind Common Sense (OMCS) project (Speer et al., 2008) started the acquisition of common sense knowledge from contributions over the web, leading to CONCEPTNET, which now also includes expert-created resources (such as WordNet) and automatically extracted knowledge or knowledge obtained through games with a purpose (Speer et al., 2008). The current version, CONCEPTNET 5.6, comprises 37 relations, some of which are commonly used in other resources like WordNet (e.g. ISA, PARTOF) while most others are more specific to capturing commonsense information and as such are particular to CONCEPTNET (e.g. HASPREREQUISITE, MOTIVATEDBYGOAL). With very few exceptions (e.g., SYNONYM or ANTONYM), CONCEPTNET-relations are asymmetric. The English version consists of 1.9 million concepts and 1.1 million links to other databases, such as DBpedia. In our work we focus on the English OMCS subpart (CN-OMCS).

3.2 Task Definition

Given a pair of concepts $\langle c_i, c_j \rangle$, where c_i, c_j may be multi-word expressions, the task is to automatically predict one (or several, see §3.3.2 for the multi-label aspect of the task) commonsense relations r_t from a given set of CONCEPTNET relation types R_{CN} that hold between c_i and c_j. Relations are presented to the classifier without textual context, and thus a crucial aspect is using a representation that properly captures the semantics of the arguments.

3.3 Designing a Relation Classification System for CONCEPTNET

CONCEPTNET has very specific properties in terms of the relations included, the type of the arguments, coverage and completeness. A successful relation classification system should take these into account. Given the heterogeneity of sources of CONCEPTNET, we focus on its core part, in particular CN-OMCS-CLN, a subset selected from CN-OMCS that includes ca. 180K triples from 36 relation types, restricted to known vocabulary from the GoogleNews Corpus (see §4.1 for further details).

3.3.1 Representing the Inputs

Word embeddings have been shown to provide useful semantic representations, capturing lexical properties of words and relative positioning in semantic space (Mikolov et al., 2013b), which has been exploited for semantic relation classification (Vylomova et al., 2016; Attia et al., 2016).

Following this work, we represent a *pair of concepts* $\langle c_i, c_j \rangle$ whose relation we want to classify through their embeddings v_{c_i} and v_{c_j}. These argument representations can be combined by subtraction $(v_{\mathrm{c_i}} - v_{\mathrm{c_j}})$ (*DiffVec*; cf. wee , rol), addition $v_{\mathrm{c_i}} + v_{\mathrm{c_j}}$ (*AddVec*) or concatenation $[v_{\mathrm{c_i}}, v_{\mathrm{c_j}}]$ (*ConcatVec*, cf. bar).

One of the issues in using such representations for CONCEPTNET is the fact that most CONCEPTNET concepts are multi-word expressions (1.93 words on average, cf. Table 2). We experiment with two ways of producing a representation for a multi-word concept: (i) computing a *centroid vector*, as the normalized sum over the embedding vectors of all words in the expression (as the baseline); (ii) encoding the expression using an RNN, e.g. a (Bi)LSTM, which encodes sequences of various lengths into one fixed-length vector. We hypothesize that using an RNN yields better concept representations than centroid vectors.

3.3.2 Constructing a Multi-Label Classifier

An important characteristic of CONCEPTNET is that more than one relation can hold for a given pair of concepts. On average this applies to 5.37% of instances per relation (cf. 2). Consequently, we cast our classification task as a *multi-label classification problem.*

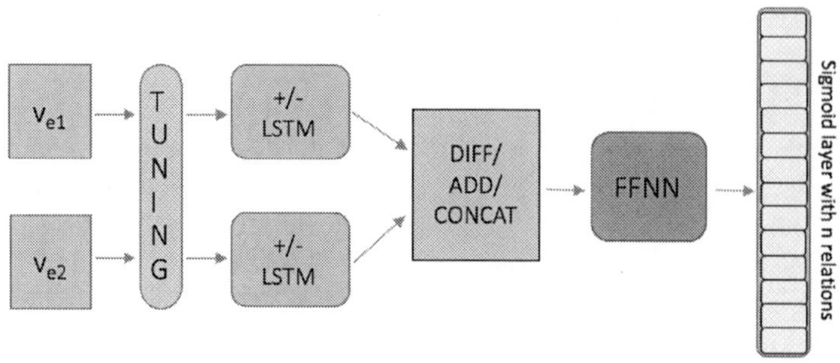

Figure 1: Multi-Label Classification Model.

Model architecture. Fig. 1 illustrates the model architecture. Input concept pairs are encoded – as centroids or using RNNs – and the representations are combined and presented to a feed-forward neural network (FFNN) with one hidden layer to non-linearly separate the relation classes.

In single-label classification, the probability for a class is not independent from the other class probabilities. Hence, $softmax$ is typically used at the output layer. By contrast, in multi-label classification, we want to model class predictions individually. The $sigmoid$ models the probability of a label as an independent *Bernoulli* distribution:

$$sig(t) = \frac{1}{1+e^{-t}} = \frac{1}{2}(1 + tanh\frac{t}{2})$$

This actually translates to an independent binary neural network for each label, resulting in a set of isolated binary classification tasks (cf. Sterbak 2017; He and Xia 2018).

The FFNN uses $sigmoid(\sigma(xW^h)W^o)$,where x is the input vector and W^h and W^o are weight matrices. We use binary cross entropy as our loss function. The architecture allows us to tune pre-trained embeddings for our relation learning task.
The hypotheses arising from the multi-label setting of CONCEPTNET are: (i) discrimination of overlapping classes is more difficult, compared to the usual relation classification task with disjoint relations (e.g. Hendrickx et al. 2010). (ii) given the incompleteness of CONCEPTNET, the classification performance may be erroneously assessed due to missing relations in the data. We will estimate the effect of this phenomenon in a small-scale annotation experiment.

3.3.3 Relation Classification Difficulty and Relation-specific Thresholding

CONCEPTNET relation types show great divergence with respect to their argument's semantic and phrase types, as shown in 2. About half of the relation arguments are nominal, entity-denoting concepts, with location as a specific entity type, half of them are event-type arguments. Several relations take different semantic types in a single argument position (e.g., HASSUBEVENT, CAUSES). Diversity of semantic types and phrase types – especially within a single argument position – is a challenge for relation learning. We expect classification to be more difficult on relations with a mixture of argument types. Because of this, different thresholds may be needed for predicting different relation types. We adopt a customized multi-label prediction setup where we tune thresholds separately for each relation type. We expect that individually tuned, relation-specific thresholds improve overall classification performance.

USEDFOR	33290	HASPREREQ.	16565	HASPROP.	5782	HAS1SUB.	2697
ATLOCATION	23874	ISA	15063	REC.ACTION	4494	DESIRES	2584
HASSUBEVENT	20518	CAUSES	12414	HASA	4118		
CAPABLEOF	18909	MOT.BYGOAL	7243	CAUSESDES.	3587		

Table 1: Number of instances per 14 most frequent relations in CN-OMCS-CLN.

relations	semantic type ARG1	semantic type ARG2	phrase type ARG1	phrase type ARG2	multiword concepts (%)	words per concept (avg)	multi-label relations (%)
IsA	entity	entity	NP	NP	46.01	1.78	1.17
HasA	entity	entity	NP	NP	56.36	1.96	1.07
AtLocation	entity	location	NP	NP	34.66	1.42	1.06
HasProperty	entity	property	NP	AP	41.41	1.80	1.31
UsedFor	entity	event	NP	VP	63.98	1.95	4.41
CapableOf	entity	event	NP	VP	58.21	1.89	1.17
ReceivesAction	entity	event	NP	VP	57.78	2.24	0.18
CausesDesire	entity	event	NP	VP	74.35	2.10	0.67
Desires	entity	ev/entity	VP	V/NP	40.02	1.68	2.79
Motiv.ByGoal	event	event	VP	VP	79.33	2.21	6.57
HasPrerequisite	event	event	VP	VP	80.27	2.23	9.86
HasFirstSubev.	event	ev/entity	VP	V/NP	83.89	2.27	36.26
HasSubevent	event	ev/entity	VP	V/NP	80.21	2.21	11.02
Causes	ev/entity	ev/entity	V/NP	V/NP	73.42	2.10	12.47
All relations					61.01	1.93	5.37

Table 2: 14 most frequent relations in CN-OMCS-CLN: their semantic and phrase types (col. 2-5); percentage of multiword concepts (col. 6); average number of words per concept (col. 7); percentage of relation instances for which we find another relation instance in CN-OMCS-CLN (col. 8).

4 Experiments

4.1 Dataset Construction

CN-OMCS-CLN CN-OMCS contains noise in form of typos, unknown words, or words from other languages than English.[1] We check all relation triples in CN-OMCS against the vocabulary of *word2vec* embeddings trained on part of the Google News dataset.[2] This embedding set contains vectors for 3 million words and phrases. We discard all relation triples from CN-OMCS which contain words that do not appear in this set. The resulting dataset – CN-OMCS-CLN – contains 179.693 triples drawn from 36 different relations (relation distribution displayed in Table 1). The OTHER class comprises all relations from CN-OMCS-CLN with less than 2000 instances.

CN-OMCS-14 Based on CN-OMCS-CLN we construct our experimental dataset CN-OMCS-14 – a balanced dataset still large enough for applying neural methods. We include all relations from CN-OMCS-CLN with more than 2000 instances, and downsample to the least frequent class – 2586 instances per relation. To select the "best" instances for testing and tuning, we sort the relation triples by their confidence score, as provided by CONCEPTNET. Inspired by Li et al. (2016) we select the 10% (258) most confident tuples per relation for testing, the next 10% for development, the remaining 80% (2068) for training, cf. Table 3.

Closed vs. Open World Setting. Learning to classify relations in a closed world setting is limited to the relation types present in the data. We want to design a system that is also able to detect whether *a relation exists* between concepts – but none of the provided ones, or whether *no relation* holds. We thus extend the data set with two classes: **OTHER** – containing concept pairs that *do stand* in a relation, yet not any of those present in the target relation set; and **RANDOM** – containing concept pairs that are *not related*.

Instances for the OTHER class consist of a sample of triples from the 22 low-frequency relations that were not included in CN-OMCS-14, these are the following relations: MADEOF, DBPEDIA, RELATEDTO, DIFFERENCE, LOCATEDNEAR, CREATEDBY, NOTUSEDFOR, FORMOF, DERIVEDFROM, OBSTRUCTEDBY, SYNONYM, PARTOF, SYMBOLOF, NOTDESIRES, HASCONTEXT, DEFINEDAS,

[1] We find a lot of Chinese words with the English tag *en* in CN-OMCS.

[2] About 100 billion words, cf. Mikolov et al. 2013a.

dataset	relations	train	dev	test
CN-OMCS-14 CW	14	28,952	3612	3612
CN-OMCS-14 OW-1	14+1	30,960	3870	3870
CN-OMCS-14 OW-2	14+2	33,088	4128	4128

Table 3: Dataset details and splits.

HASLASTSUBEVENT, EXTERNALURL, INSTANCEOF, NOTCAPABLEOF, and NOTHASPROPERTY.

Instances for the RANDOM class are generated similarly to Vylomova et al. (2016): 50% of instances are *opposite pairs*, obtained by switching the order of concept pairs within the same relation; 50% are *corrupt pairs*, obtained by replacing one concept in a connected pair with a random concept from the same relation. Using *corrupt pairs* ensures that our model does not simply learn properties of the word classes, but instead is forced to encode relation instances. RANDOM and OTHER are the same size as the individual target relations.

4.2 Experiment Setup

Experiments and Datasets. We experiment with two open world settings: in OW-1 we add only the RANDOM class to CN-OMCS-14, to investigate whether the classifier is able to differentiate related from non-related concept pairs. in OW-2 we add both OTHER and RANDOM to CN-OMCS-14, to investigate whether the classifier can also learn to predict that an unknown relation exists or that no relation holds. We also report results of the closed world setting where we exclude OTHER and RANDOM. Each dataset is split into training (80%), dev (10%) and test (10%) (cf. Table 3).
Evaluation. We evaluate model performance in terms of F1 score for each relation. We report averaged weighted F1 scores over 5 runs.

4.3 Model Parameters

Embeddings. Based on preliminary experiments[3], we use 300-dim. skip-gram *word2vec* embeddings trained on part of the Google News dataset (100 billion words, Mikolov et al. 2013a). Embeddings are tuned during training.
Concept representation. Concept are encoded using centroid vectors or an RNN (cf. §3.3.1).
Relation representation. We use the *ConcatVec* representation (§3.3.1), which we determined to be the most useful in preliminary experiments.
Label prediction thresholds are tuned in two ways: (i) a global threshold for all relations and (ii) separately tuned thresholds for each relation.
Hyperparameter settings were determined on the devset. For encoding of multiword terms we use bi-LSTMs with one hidden layer and a cell size of 350 (perform better than GRUs and LSTMs). For the FFNN we tune the hidden layer size and the activation function. Optimal hyperparameters are 200 (FFNN), 100 (FFNN+RNN), and $ReLU$ for both FFNN and FFNN+RNN.
Implementation. We implemented our models with *PyTorch* (Paszke et al., 2017).

4.4 Results

Table 4 summarizes the results in open (OW) and closed world (CW) settings.

The overall best performing model across all settings is FFNN+RNN (as opposed to FFNN with centroid argument representations) with relation-specific label prediction thresholds (as opposed to one global threshold value). In the OW setting we achieve overall F1-scores of 0.68 (OW-1) and 0.65 (OW-2). The CW setting leads to best results with 0.71 F1. The models improve by 4pp (OW-1), 7pp (OW-2) and

[3]We additionally tested Numberbatch embeddings (Speer et al., 2017), GloVe embeddings trained on Wikipedia and Gigaword (Pennington et al., 2014), context2vec embeddings trained on UkWaC (Melamud et al., 2016). In our experiments we discovered that all of these alternatives perform worse than the *word2vec* embeddings.

Setting	OpenWorld OW-1		OpenWorld OW-2		Closed World	
Model	FF	FF+RNN	FF	FF+RNN	FF	FF+RNN
IsA	.58 (.57)	.62 (.60)	.51 (.51)	.60 (.57)	.64 (.63)	.67 (.67)
HasA	.67 (.66)	.80 (.79)	.53 (.52)	.79 (.77)	.73 (.72)	.80 (.78)
AtLocation	.69 (.68)	.78 (.78)	.63 (.61)	.74 (.72)	.77 (.75)	.84 (.83)
HasProperty	.66 (.65)	.81 (.80)	.62 (.61)	.78 (.77)	.67 (.67)	.84 (.83)
UsedFor	.76 (.75)	.78 (.77)	.79 (.78)	.76 (.76)	.78 (.78)	.79 (.78)
CapableOf	.61 (.61)	.67 (.65)	.56 (.56)	.65 (.64)	.61 (.60)	.71 (.71)
ReceivesAction	.82 (.82)	.91 (.91)	.77 (.77)	.90 (.90)	.87 (.86)	.93 (.93)
Caus.Des.	.87 (.87)	.90 (.88)	.86 (.85)	.87 (.87)	.87 (.86)	.92 (.90)
Desires	.91 (.85)	.94 (.92)	.73 (.65)	.93 (.88)	.87 (.83)	.88 (.94)
MoticatedByGoal	.61 (.60)	.56 (.55)	.56 (.55)	.59 (.59)	.60 (.59)	.64 (.61)
HasPrerequisite	.45 (.41)	.38 (.36)	.38 (.36)	.38 (.36)	.43 (.42)	.39 (.38)
HasFirstSubevent	.54 (.53)	.55 (.55)	.49 (.49)	.56 (.55)	.51 (.50)	.61 (.60)
HasSubevent	.24 (.22)	.26 (.16)	.17 (.15)	.24 (.15)	.21 (.21)	.24 (.20)
Causes	.60 (.59)	.57 (.56)	.59 (.58)	.61 (.60)	.61 (.60)	.61 (.61)
Other	-	-	.39 (.39)	.40 (.40)	-	-
Random	.61 (.58)	.59 (.54)	.62 (.61)	.53 (.49)	-	-
Weighted F1	.64 (.63)	.68 (.66)	.58 (.56)	.65 (.63)	.65 (.64)	.71 (.69)

Table 4: Weighted F1 results on Cn-Omcs-14. Main results obtained with relation-specific prediction thresholds (in brackets: results for global prediction threshold).

	multi word terms (%)	words/term (avg)	multi-label rel.(%)		multi word terms (%)	words/term (avg)	multi-label rel.(%)
IsA	43.43	1.72	1.70	HasA	55.37	1.88	0.46
AtLocation	36.02	1.43	1.86	HasProperty	40.21	1.75	0.62
UsedFor	64.38	1.90	3.25	CapableOf	55.91	1.83	2.86
ReceivesAction	55.91	2.21	0.15	CausesDesire	74.33	2.09	0.23
Desires	40.11	1.68	2.01	MotivatedByGoal	78.46	2.16	5.19
HasPrerequisite	77.88	2.15	13.70	HasFirstSubevent	84.78	2.30	10.84
HasSubevent	79.23	2.20	14.94	Causes	72.11	2.04	4.18
Other	53.49	1.82	9.52	Random	55.21	1.84	0

Table 5: Relation statistics on Cn-Omcs-14. Results for all relations (Ow-1): 60.01 % of MW terms, 1.94 (average number of words/term), and 4.77 % of relation instances with multiple labels.

6pp (CW) when replacing centroids with bi-LSTM encoded concept representations. Relation-specific thresholds improve results by 2pp (FFNN+RNN on OW-1, OW-2 and CW). Across all settings (CW, OW-1, OW-2) the best performing relations are: Desires (0.94), ReceivesAction (0.91), CausesDesire (0.90). We observe lowest F1-scores for HasSubevent (0.26, 0.24), HasPrerequisite (0.38, 0.39) and HasFirstSubevent (0.55, 0.61) in OW-1 and CW, respectively. The random and other classes have poor results overall. OW-2 with two OW classes performs worse than OW-1 with the single random class. The low results on the other class (0.40) could stem from its heterogeneity. The system finds it difficult to differentiate other and random.

5 Analysis

In this section we will discuss the hypotheses derived from our analysis of ConceptNet properties (§3.3), and based on that, to determine which approaches and representations are best suited for ConceptNet-based commonsense relation classification. To aid the discussion we produced Figures 2, 3, 4, and Table 5.

Fig. 2 plots differences in performance for each relation for the setting we wish to compare: *concept encoding* using centroids (FFnn) vs. RNNs (FFnn+Rnn) (blue), *global vs. relation-specific* prediction threshold (orange), and OW-1 vs. CW setting (grey).

Fig. 3 visualizes ambiguous – that means co-occurring – relations in our dataset in a symmetric heatmap.

Fig. 4 displays interrelations between concept characteristics and model performance, based on our best performing system (FFNN+RNN+ind. tuned thresholds, OW-1). To observe correlations between clas-

sification performance and different measurable characteristics of the data in Fig. 4, we scaled the following values for each relation to a common range of 0 to 15: the percentage of multi-word terms (cf. Table 2) (grey), the average number of words per concept (cf. Table 2) (yellow), percentage of relation instances with multiple labels (cf. Table 2) (blue), best model performance on OW-1 (FFNN+RNN with individually tuned thresholds, cf. Table 4) (red) and the corresponding relation-specific thresholds (green).
Table 5 gives relation statistics on CN-OMCS-14 (as opposed to Table 2, which gives statistics for the complete version CN-OMCS-CLN).

5.1 Representing Multi-word Concepts

We hypothesized that there is a correlation between the length of the arguments and model performance when encoding arguments with an RNN. We find no such correlation – the relations that benefit the most from using an RNN (Fig. 2: blue and Fig. 4: yellow, red) are not those with the longest arguments (cf. Table 5). Instead we find that the relations HASPROPERTY, HASA, ATLOCATION, and RECEIVESACTION benefit most from concept encoding with a RNN, followed by CAPABLEOF, ISA, DESIRES, CAUSES-DESIRE and HAS(FIRST)SUBEVENT with lower margins. The missing correlation can be confirmed by a very low Pearson's coefficient of only 0.05 between (1) improvements we get from enhancing FFNN with RNN (i.e., delta of F1 scores for FFNN vs. FFNN+RNN; both with individually tuned thresholds) and (2) the average number of words per concepts (cf. Table 2).

5.2 Threshold Tuning & Model Performance

We hypothesized that relations would benefit from having individually tuned thresholds. Overall, the models with RNN encoding of concepts benefit more from threshold tuning than the basic FFNN. Regarding single relations (Fig. 2, orange bars), HASSUBEVENT and the open world class RANDOM benefit the most from individual threshold tuning (both with relatively low F1 scores). The individual thresholds vary considerably across relations (Fig. 4).

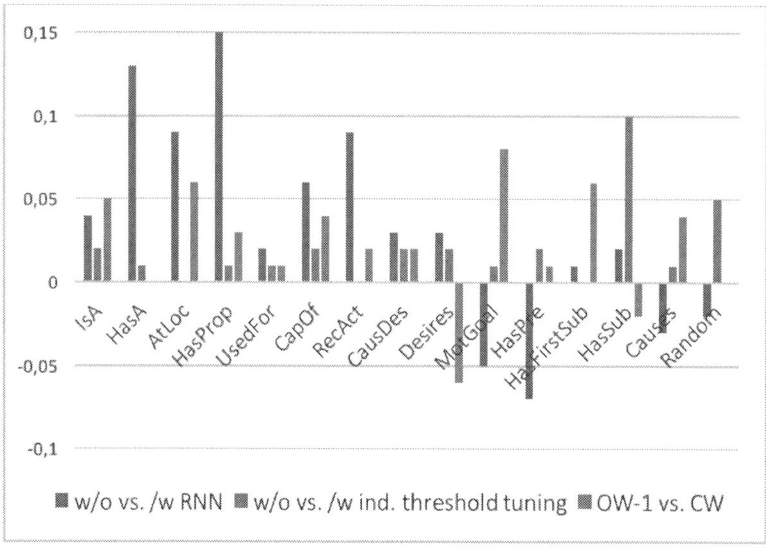

Figure 2: Delta of F1-scores on CN-OMCS-14: (i) FFNN vs. FFNN+RNN: (relation-specific threshold, OW-1, blue); (ii) global vs. relation-specific threshold (FFNN+RNN,OW-1, orange); (iii) OW-1 vs. CW (FFNN+RNN, relation-specific threshold, grey).

To test whether relations that are harder to classify benefit the most from tuning the threshold (as the performance of HASSUBEVENT and RANDOM seem to indicate), we compute the correlation between (1) the difference of model performance with and without individually tuned thresholds (as described above) and (2) general model performance (F1 scores of FFNN+RNN with global threshold, OW-1). The score of -0.67 Pearson correlation indicates that indeed relations with lower general performance will tend to have higher improvements. This is also reflected in Fig. 4 (green and red), which also shows that for relations with higher F1 scores, higher thresholds tend to work better. Relation classification models applied to CONCEPTNET should therefore have higher thresholds for relations with high classification confidence (high F1 scores), while for relations with low performance lower thresholds are recommended.

5.3 Closed vs. Open World Setting

Most relations perform better in the CW setting (cf. grey bars in Fig. 2), especially MOTIVATEDBYGOAL, HASFIRSTSUBEVENT, ATLOCATION, and ISA (Fig. 2, grey). In contrast, DESIRES and HASSUBEVENT perform better in an open world setting (Fig. 2). Comparing the two settings OW-1 and OW-2 (Table 4, not displayed in Fig. 2), we find that only the relations MOTIVATEDBY, HASFIRSTSUBEVENT and CAUSES perform better in OW-2 than in OW-1. All other relations benefit from the OW-1 setting, especially ATLOCATION and the open world class RANDOM.

5.4 Relation Heterogeneity

We hypothesized that relations that are more heterogeneous with respect to the type of their arguments (whether semantic or phrasal) will be harder to learn. Comparing the degree of diversity of semantic or phrase types (Table 2) with model performance confirms this hypothesis. The relations that perform best have semantically or "phrasally" consistent arguments, whereas (apart from DESIRE) relation types that feature different types of entities or phrases in the same argument position tend to achieve low F1 scores.

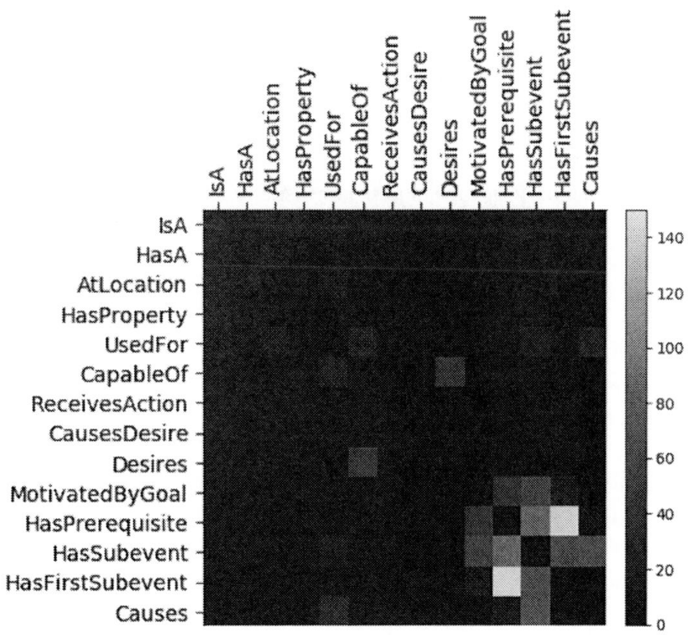

Figure 3: Visualizing ambiguous (co-occurring) relations in CN-OMCS-14 in a symmetric heatmap.

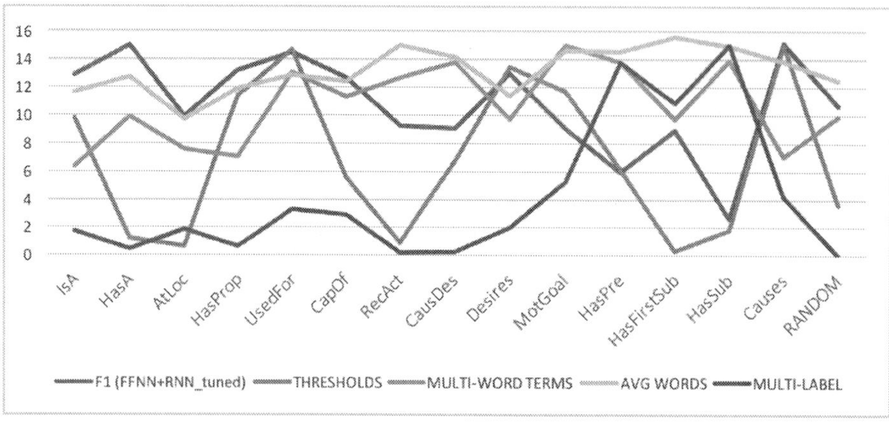

Figure 4: Interrelations between concept characteristics and model performance, based on FFNN+RNN+individually tuned thresholds, OW-1, scaled to range 0 to 15.

5.5 Relation Ambiguity

We hypothesized that relations that have multi-labeled instances (instances to which more than one label – relation – applies) will be more difficult to learn. Fig. 3 illustrates relation co-occurrences, i.e. relations that have overlapping instances. The most frequently co-occuring relations in CN-OMCS-14 are HASPREREQUISITE & HASFIRSTSUBEVENT, (150 co-occurrences), HASSUBEVENT & HASPREREQUISITE (90) and HASSUBEVENT & OTHER (86).[4] 399 concept pairs have two relation labels (e.g., ⟨*a cat,meow*⟩: DESIRES, CAPABLEOF), 20 pairs have three (e.g., ⟨*playing a harp,making music*⟩: CAUSES, HASSUBEVENT, USEDFOR), and two pairs have four: ⟨*opening a gift,surprise*⟩: HASPREREQUISITE, CAUSES, HASSUBEVENT, USEDFOR.

Fig. 4 shows a strong inverse correlation (-0.82 Pearson) between model performance and the number of multi-labeled instances for that relation.

5.6 Favorable vs. Unfavorable Properties of CONCEPTNET

We have investigated several variations of a relation classification model, each variation designed to mitigate some particular feature of CONCEPTNET relations. Analysis of these models have shown what impact each has on the model performance, and which issues we could address and which we could not. One of the issues was the length of the arguments. Using an RNN that can encode such sequences of various lengths did not lead to consistent improvements for relations with long arguments. The classifier still performs best on relations with short arguments. However, we do obtain overall better results with RNN encoding of arguments.

Another issue was the heterogeneity of relations in terms of the semantic or phrasal type of their arguments. The analysis has shown that indeed such relations suffer during classification, but individual tuning of the threshold partly helps.

One of the most striking challenges posed by the CONCEPTNET relation inventory remains the observed relation ambiguity. Here, our analysis matches our hypothesis, which was that multi-relation instances are harder to classify than relations for which we rarely find relation instances which co-occur with other relation labels. We further find that individual threshold tuning helps improving classification performance, especially for relations which are harder to classify and are characterized by low F1 scores. These are again exactly the relations which usually show other challenging properties including relation ambiguity, long arguments, and inner-relation diversity regarding concept and phrasal types.

[4]In CN-OMCS-CLN (complete, unbalanced dataset) the most frequently overlapping relations are: USEDFOR & CAUSES (800), HASSUBEVENT & CAUSES (636), and HASSUBEVENT & HASPREREQUISITE (628).

5.7 Impact of Missing Edges

The ambiguity of ConceptNet relations combined with the incompleteness of the resource pose challenges for evaluating the performance of a model. A classification decision marked as false positive could in fact be valid. This issue penalizes single-label and multi-label classifiers differently: a single-label classifier is not allowed to predict multiple labels, while a multi-label classifier will learn from potentially false negatives and depending on the distribution of the data could learn to over-predict. To investigate to what degree this issue impacts the results of our model, we manually annotate a small sample of the test data and compare it to the gold standard.

Annotation Experiment. We performed a small annotation experiment in which we manually control a subset of 200 instances from our test set for missing edges. Our sample consists of concept pairs which are related with one of the 14 relations in Cn-Omcs-14, and we want to investigate if another, additional relation holds between the two concepts. We therefore present the concept pair and a randomly sampled relation from our relation set (excluding the gold label) to two annotators without showing the gold label. We ask them if the relation applies or not, and they are also allowed to assign *Not Sure* as a third option. The annotators agreed in 178 of 200 instances (91%). The annotations are merged by a third expert annotator. In the final gold version 18 (9%) of the instances are labelled as applicable (e.g. ⟨*cook dinner*,HasPrerequisite,*turn on stove*⟩), while 176 (88%) don't apply according to the annotators (e.g. ⟨*coffee*,HasSubevent,*popular drink*⟩). According to this small annotated subset, we conclude that a lower bound of almost 9% of the predictions could be penalized due to incompleteness of the ConceptNet resource or our extracted subset, respectively. Of course this has to be verified in an annotation experiment of a larger scale.

6 Conclusion

In this paper we investigated several variations of a multi-label neural relational classifier for ConceptNet relations. Each variation was designed to account for specific properties of ConceptNet. An in-depth study revealed specific characteristics that can make ConceptNet relation classification difficult: several distinct relation types may hold for a given concept pair; some relations have heterogeneous arguments; and many concepts are expressed through multi-word terms. In light of these challenges posed by the specific properties of ConceptNet, we design a multi-label classification model which uses RNNs for representing multi-word arguments and individually tuned thresholds for improving model performance, especially for relations with unfavorable properties such as long arguments, relation ambiguity and inner-relation diversity. Our best performing model achieves F1 scores of 68 in an open world and 71 in a closed world setting. The analysis of the results in different configurations shows that the design decisions driven by multi-word representations and threshold tuning improved the overall classification performance, and that our model is able to tackle specific properties of ConceptNet. Yet, some challenges could not be resolved and need to be addressed in future work. In particular this concerns relation ambiguity and heterogeneity of relation arguments. The observed co-occurences of relations could be deployed for targeting relation ambiguity by building a meta classifier which learns which relations can or cannot occur together.

In future work, we plan to use the multi-label classification system proposed in this paper for enriching ConceptNet by predicting relations between concepts which are not yet linked in the network. Our investigation can further inform and caution the community on both the usefulness and the flaws of this resource and guide future work on using ConceptNet.

Acknowledgements. This work has been funded by Deutsche Forschungsgemeinschaft within the project *ExpLAIN. Between the Lines – Knowledge-based Analysis of Argumentation in a Formal Argumentation Inference System*, FR 1707/-4-1, as part of the RATIO Priority Program. We also want to thank our reviewers, our annotators Angel Daza and Esther van den Berg, and NVIDIA for donating GPUs.

References

Mohammed Attia, Suraj Maharjan, Younes Samih, Laura Kallmeyer, and Thamar Solorio. 2016. CogALex-V Shared Task: GHHH - Detecting Semantic Relations via Word Embeddings. In *Proceedings of the 5th Workshop on Cognitive Aspects of the Lexicon (CogALex - V)*, pages 86–91.

Huihui He and Rui Xia. 2018. Joint Binary Neural Network for Multi-label Learning with Applications to Emotion Classification. *7th CCF International Conference. Hohhot, China.*, pages 250–259.

Iris Hendrickx, Su Nam Kim, Zornitsa Kozareva, Preslav Nakov, Diarmuid Ó Séaghdha, Sebastian Padó, Marco Pennacchiotti, Lorenza Romano, and Stan Szpakowicz. 2010. SemEval-2010 Task 8: Multi-Way Classification of Semantic Relations between Pairs of Nominals. In *Proceedings of the 5th International Workshop on Semantic Evaluation*, pages 33–38, Uppsala, Sweden. Association for Computational Linguistics.

José-Angel González and Hurtado Oliver, Lluís and Segarra, Encarna and Pla, Ferran. 2018. ELiRF-UPV at SemEval-2018 Task 11: Machine Comprehension using Commonsense Knowledge. In *Proceedings of The 12th International Workshop on Semantic Evaluation*, pages 1034–1037.

Dieu Thu Le, J Uijlings, and Raffaella Bernardi. 2013. Exploiting Language Models For Visual Recognition. *EMNLP 2013 - Conference on Empirical Methods in Natural Language Processing, Proceedings of the Conference*, pages 769–779.

Xiang Li, Aynaz Taheri, Lifu Tu, and Kevin Gimpel. 2016. Commonsense Knowledge Base Completion. In *Proceedings of the 54th Annual Meeting of the Association for Computational Linguistics (Volume 1: Long Papers)*, pages 1445–1455, Berlin, Germany. Association for Computational Linguistics.

Henry Liebermann. 2008. Usable AI Requires Commonsense Knowledge. In *Workshop on Usable artificial intelligence, held in conjunction with the Conference on Human Factors in Computing Systems (CHI)*.

Oren Melamud, Jacob Goldberger, and Ido Dagan. 2016. Context2Vec: Learning Generic Context Embedding with Bidirectional LSTM. In *CoNLL*, pages 51–61. Association for Computational Linguistics.

Todor Mihaylov and Anette Frank. 2018. Knowledgeable Reader: Enhancing Cloze-Style Reading Comprehension with External Common Knowledge. In *Proceedings of the 56th Annual Meeting of the Association for Computational Linguistics*, Melbourne, Australia. Association for Computational Linguistics.

Tomas Mikolov, Ilya Sutskever, Kai Chen, Greg Corrado, and Jeffrey Dean. 2013a. Distributed Representations of Words and Phrases and Their Compositionality. In *Proceedings of the 26th International Conference on Neural Information Processing Systems - Volume 2*, pages 3111–3119, USA. Curran Associates Inc.

Tomas Mikolov, Scott Wen-tau Yih, and Geoffrey Zweig. 2013b. Linguistic Regularities in Continuous Space Word Representations. In *Proceedings of the 2013 Conference of the North American Chapter of the Association for Computational Linguistics: Human Language Technologies (NAACL-HLT-2013)*. Association for Computational Linguistics.

Vivi Nastase, Preslav Nakov, Diarmuid O Seaghdha, and Stan Szpakowicz. 2013. Semantic Relations between Nominals. *Synthesis lectures on human language technologies*, 6(1):1–119.

Simon Ostermann, Michael Roth, Ashutosh Modi, Stefan Thater, and Manfred Pinkal. 2018. SemEval-2018 Task 11: Machine Comprehension Using Commonsense Knowledge. In *Proceedings of The 12th International Workshop on Semantic Evaluation*, pages 747–757. Association for Computational Linguistics.

Adam Paszke, Sam Gross, and Adam Lerer. 2017. Automatic differentiation in PyTorch. In *Workshop Autodiff: The future of gradient-based machine learning software and techniques. Collocated with NIPS 2017.*

Jeffrey Pennington, Richard Socher, and Christopher D Manning. 2014. Glove: Global Vectors for Word Representation. In *Conference on Empirical Methods in Natural Language Processing (EMNLP)*, volume 14, pages 1532–1543.

Feiliang Ren, Di Zhou, Zhihui Liu, Yongcheng Li, Rongsheng Zhao, Yongkang Liu, and Xiaobo Liang. 2018. Neural Relation Classification with Text Descriptions. In *Proceedings of the 27th International Conference on Computational Linguistics*, pages 1167–1177. Association for Computational Linguistics.

Itsumi Saito, Kyosuke Nishida, Hisako Asano, and Junji Tomita. 2018. Commonsense Knowledge Base Completion and Generation. In *Proceedings of the 22nd Conference on Computational Natural Language Learning*, pages 141–150. Association for Computational Linguistics.

Seiya Shudo, Rafal Rzepka, and Kenji Araki. 2016. Automatic Evaluation of Commonsense Knowledge for Refining Japanese ConceptNet. *Proceedings of the 12th Workshop on Asian Language Resources*, pages 105–112.

Robert Speer, Joshua Chin, and Catherine Havasi. 2017. ConceptNet 5.5: An Open Multilingual Graph of General Knowledge. *Proceedings of 31St AAAI Conference on Artificial Intelligence.*

Robert Speer, Catherine Havasi, and Henry Lieberman. 2008. AnalogySpace: Reducing the Dimensionality of Common Sense Knowledge. In *Proceedings of the 23rd National Conference on Artificial Intelligence - Volume 1*, pages 548–553. AAAI Press.

Tobias Sterbak. 2017. Guide To Multi-Class Multi-Label Classification With Neural Networks In Python. *Blogpost: https://www.depends-on-the-definition.com/guide-to-multi-label-classification-with-neural-networks/.*

Zhen Tan, Bo Li, Peixin Huang, Bin Ge, and Weidong Xiao. 2018. Neural Relation Classification Using Selective Attention and Symmetrical Directional Instances. *Symmetry*, 10:357.

Ekaterina Vylomova, Laura Rimell, Trevor Cohn, and Timothy Baldwin. 2016. Take and Took, Gaggle and Goose, Book and Read: Evaluating the Utility of Vector Differences for Lexical Relation Learning. In *Proceedings of the 54th Annual Meeting of the Association for Computational Linguistics (Volume 1: Long Papers)*, pages 1671–1682, Berlin, Germany. Association for Computational Linguistics.

Zhigang Wang and Juanzi Li. 2018. Three-way Attention and Relational Knowledge for Commonsense Machine Comprehension. In *Proceedings of The 12th International Workshop on Semantic Evaluation*. Association for Computational Linguistics.

Dirk Weissenborn, Tomas Kocisky, and Chris Dyer. 2018. Dynamic Integration of Background Knowledge in Neural NLU Systems. *ICLR 2018.*

Tom Young, Erik Cambria, Iti Chaturvedi, Hao Zhou, Subham Biswas, and Minlie Huang. 2018. Augmenting End-to-End Dialog Systems with Commonsense Knowledge. *AAAI 2018*.

Xiaobin Zhang, Fucai Chen, and Ruiyang Huang. 2018. A Combination of RNN and CNN for Attention-based Relation Classification. In *Procedia Computer Science*, volume 131, pages 911 – 917.

Detecting Collocations Similarity via Logical-Linguistic Model

Nina Khairova, Svitlana Petrasova
National Technical University "Kharkiv Polytechnic Institute",
Kyrpychova str., 61002, Kharkiv, Ukraine
khairova@kpi.kharkov.ua, svetapetrasova@gmail.com

Orken Mamyrbayev
Institute of Information and Computational Technologies,
125, Pushkin str., 050010, Almaty, Republic of Kazakhstan
morkenj@mail.ru

Kuralay Mukhsina
Al-Farabi Kazakh National University,
71 al-Farabi Ave., Almaty, Republic of Kazakhstan,
kuka_ai@mail.ru

Abstract

Semantic similarity between collocations, along with words similarity, is one of the main issues of NLP. In particular, it might be addressed to facilitate the automatic thesaurus generation. In the paper, we consider the logical-linguistic model that allows defining the relation of semantic similarity of collocations via the logical-algebraic equations. We provide the model for English, Ukrainian and Russian text corpora. The implementation for each language is slightly different in the equations of the finite predicates algebra and used linguistic resources. As a dataset for our experiment, we use 5801 pairs of sentences of Microsoft Research Paraphrase Corpus for English and more than 1 000 texts of scientific papers for Russian and Ukrainian.

1 Introduction

Nowadays, linguistic resources are not only a part of any linguistic study but an important base for designing NLP applications such as search engines, machine (-assisted) translation, context-sensitive ads, document clustering, automatic essay scoring, business intelligence (e.g. sentiment analysis) and text summarization. Linguistic resources typically include linguistic ontologies, monolingual and multilingual corpora and various kinds of dictionaries.

Thesauri, where words are associated with semantic relations to each other, are of particular importance among all dictionary types. However, in order to create a thesaurus, lexicographic researches, the analysis of the lexical structure of languages, exploring of the text characteristics and similar labour-intensive studies must be conducted (Jarmasz and Szpakowicz, 2003). The thesaurus design process can be accelerated by the automation of the close concepts identification step.

In a general way, such concepts are represented by a single word, but sometimes a concept can be represented by two or three related words. As of today, a sufficient number of approaches exists to find and extract semantically similar words from a corpus automatically. However, measuring the semantic similarity between word groups or collocations is a more challenging task which has no satisfactory solution to date.

In our study, we propose the logical-linguistic model to identify semantic similarity of collocations. Generally, a collocation is considered as a combination of two lexical units in syntactic and semantic relations that co-occur in the text non-randomly. The probabilistic study of collocation occurrence is beyond the scope of this research, though. We assume that two-word combinations are considered as collocations if they occur more than once in synonymous meanings.

We created the models for English, Ukrainian and Russian languages. Using these models, in general, allows extracting semantically similar collocations from a text corpus automatically in order to generate a first draft of the thesaurus.

2 Related work

The most explored level of text similarity for different languages is the level of words. In this way, we can distinguish two classes of words similarity algorithms. The first approach is based on the exploitation of a thesaurus (Pirró and Seco, 2008; Pedersen et al., 2007). The second methods and algorithms group of word similarity identification focuses on distributional models of meaning in a corpus (Islam and Inkpen, 2006; Han et al., 2013; Akermi and Faiz, 2012).

There is much less research related to the measurement of similarity between sentences or short text fragments (Islam and Inkpen, 2008). In order to evaluate the degree of two English sentences semantic similarity, Sultan et al. exploited an unsupervised system that relied on word alignment (Sultan et al., 2014) or combined a vector similarity feature with alignment-based similarity (Sultan et al., 2015). Now quite a few researchers apply align words algorithms in order to compute the semantic similarity between two sentences. McCrae et al. (2016) also exploited the idea of creating monolingual alignments to assess the degree of semantic similarity of sentences. However, they proposed to use soft alignment, where they produced a score indicating how likely one word in the sentence was to be aligned to another word in the other sentence.

Dang et al. (2016), like many others, drew on tweets as short text fragments. They proposed to use Wikipedia as an external knowledge source and a corpus-based word semantic relatedness method to determine whether two tweets are semantically similar or not. Rakib et al. (2016) also benefited from an external knowledge source such as Google-n-grams. They computed relatedness strength between two phrases using the sum-ratio technique in conjunction with cosine similarity via bi-gram contexts from Google-n-grams. Recently Boom et al. (2015) used a hybrid method that united word embedding and tf-idf information of a text fragment into a distributed representation of very short text fragments semantically close to each other.

Increasingly, the task of measuring the semantic similarity of short text fragments is being integrated into the common challenges of the paraphrase. However, in general, such researches involve semantic similarity of sentences (Ganitkevitch et al., 2013; Pavlick et al., 2015). Extracting paraphrase fragment pairs, Wang and Callison-Burch (2011) used a comparable corpus, and in the next study they utilized parallel corpora considering discourse information (Regneri and Wang, 2012).

Measuring the semantic similarity of collocations is a more challenging task than searching words or sentences with similar meaning. This is connected to the fact that both identifying collocations and establishing their synonymy must be involved in the process of detecting semantically similar items.

3 The proposed method for detecting semantic similarity

We propose a method to detect and extract semantically similar collocations from text corpora. In our study, we consider semantically similar collocations as synonymous collocations with certain assumption having been made.

The method is based on the logical-linguistic model (Khairova et al., 2015) that: (1) formalizes semantic and grammatical words characteristics of prospective collocations by means of the subject variables; (2) identifies substantive, attributive and verbal collocations by means of equations of the finite predicates algebra; (3) formalizes structures of semantically similar collocations via the logical-algebraic equations. Additionally, we exploit POS-tagging and thesauri as linguistic resources of a particular language. POS-tagging is applied to extract grammatical characteristics of words, and thesauri are applied to find potential synonyms of the collocation words that were identified in the first and second phases of the model.

Fig. 1 shows the structural scheme of the method, which highlights the synergy between the logical-linguistic model and linguistic resources of a particular language.

We provide the model for extraction of semantically similar collocations from Ukrainian, Russian and English text corpora. The semantic cohesion between 2 words in a collocation is expressed by morphological and syntactic relations in all these languages. The distinctions between the implementations of the model for the various languages are in (1) different values of the subject variables, (2) slightly different logical-linguistic equations of substantive, attributive, verbal collocations and (3) discrepancy of logical-algebraic equations of the semantic similarity for collocations. The main reason for this differentiation is that the semantic cohesion in the Ukrainian and Russian languages is represented by a range of grammatical cases while the order of words and existence of prepositions represent the semantic relations in English.

In this way, the model involves the following steps. The first step is preprocessing when we tag a text corpus. POS-tagging is carried out in order to identify substantive (Noun-Noun), attributive (Adjective-Noun), and verbal (Verb-Noun) collocations. In the next step, we identify characteristics of collocation words. Furthermore, using a thesaurus we get synonymous pairs of words that were found in the previous steps. The last step, we determine pairs of semantically similar collocations using the predicates of equivalence and then find the pairs in a corpus.

In the first preprocessing stage, we perform POS-tagging by means of NLTK Python library to identify two adjacent words as a possible collocation. For example, to identify substantive (Noun-Noun) collocations in the Ukrainian language, we find the main word marked <NN >and one of the other tags, which represents the grammar case, must be <Nom >, <Gen>, <Dat>, <Acc>, <In>or <Pr>. The dependent word of substantive collocations in the Ukrainian language must be marked as a noun too (<NN >). Nevertheless, its case must be marked only as <Gen>.

In this way, substantive collocations in Ukrainian can be defined by the following logical-linguistic equation:

$$(x^{NNom} \vee x^{NGen} \vee x^{NDat} \vee x^{NAcc} \vee x^{NIn} \vee x^{NPr})y^{NGen} = 1 \tag{1}$$

Similarly, we can determine attributive and verbal collocations by the following logical-linguistic equations respectively:

$$\begin{gathered} y^{ANom}x^{NNom} \vee y^{AGen}x^{NGen} \vee y^{ADat}x^{NDat} \vee y^{AAcc}x^{NAcc} \vee \\ y^{AIn}x^{NAIn} \vee y^{APr}x^{NPr} = 1 \end{gathered} \tag{2}$$

$$x^{VNonRef}y^{NAcc} = 1 \tag{3}$$

In the equations (1)- (3) the subject variable x describes a set of possible grammatical characteristics for a main collocation word and the subject variable y describes a possible set of characteristics for a dependent word of the collocation.

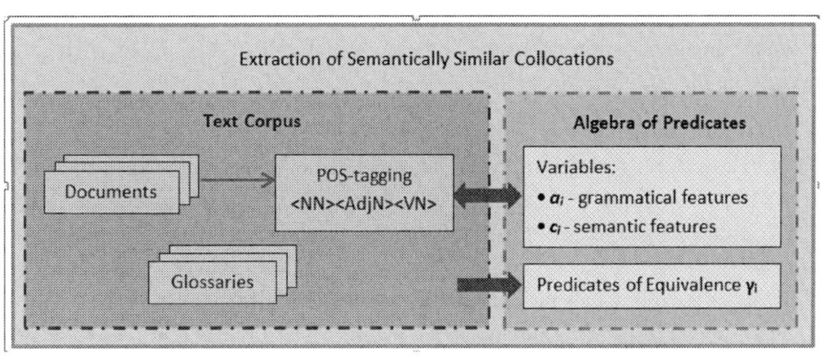

Figure 1: The structural scheme of our method

The next step, we define a set of grammatical and semantic characteristics of words for the Ukrainian, Russian, and English languages using two subject variables that define grammatical (a^i) and semantic (c^i) categories of the language. Every subject variable z^i equals to 1 if main or dependent words might have these i characteristics, and it equals to 0 otherwise. The grammatical characteristics of collocation words are mostly received as a result of POS-tagging.

As illustrated above, for Ukrainian and Russian languages the main grammatical characteristics that show the dependency in collocations are a part of speech, transitivity (in case of verbs) and a case. As for English, such grammatical characteristics, apart from POS and verb transitivity, are the existence of a particular preposition and/or the existence of the apostrophe at the end of the word and/or the existence of any form of the verb "to be" in the phrase and the position of the noun concerning a verb (Khairova et al., 2016).

The subject variable c^i defines 6 semantic cases for all three languages: c^{Ag} – an Agent, c^{Att} – an Attribute, c^{Pac} – a Patient, c^{Adr} – an Addressee, c^{Ins} – an Instrument, c^M – a Location or Content.

In our model, a set of possible grammatical and semantic characteristics for the main collocation word is defined by the predicate P(x). The predicate P(y) specifies grammatical and semantic characteristics of the dependent word in collocations. Therefore, we define two-word collocations via the double predicate P(x, y) that combines two previous predicates. For the Ukrainian and Russian languages, the predicate is following:

$$\begin{aligned} P(x,y) =&(a_y^{ANom} \vee a_y^{AGen} \vee a_y^{AAcc} \vee a_y^{ADat} \vee a_y^{AIn} \vee a_y^{APr})(a_x^{ANom} c_x^{Ag} \vee a_x^{NGen} c_x^{Att} \vee \\ &a_x^{NAcc} c_x^{Pac} \vee a_x^{NDat} c_x^{Adr} \vee a_x^{NIn} c_x^{Ins} \vee a_x^{NPr} c_x^{M}) a_y^{NGen} c_y^{Att} \vee a_x^{VNonRef} a_y^{NAcc} c_y^{Pac} \end{aligned} \tag{4}$$

While in the case of English, the predicate that identifies grammatical and semantic characteristics of words in two-word collocations is following:

$$\begin{aligned} P(x,y) =&a_y^{AAtt} a_x^{NSubj} c_x^{Ag} \vee a_x^{NSubj} c_x^{Ag} a_y^{APr} \vee (a_x^{NSubj} c_x^{Ag} \vee a_x^{NSubjOf} c_x^{Ag}) \\ &(a_x^{NObj} c_x^{Att} \vee a_x^{NObjOf} c_x^{Att}) \vee a_x^{VNonRef} a_y^{NObj} c_y^{Pac} \end{aligned} \tag{5}$$

For example, the correlation of semantic and grammatical characteristics of Ukrainian attributive collocations such as "technical facilities" ("tekhnichni zasoby") or "engineering tools" ("inzhenerni instrumenty") satisfies the conjunction $a_y^{ANom} a_x^{NNom} c_x^{Ag}$ of the predicate (4). The English word combinations "form the notion" or "create the view" satisfies the conjunction of the grammatical and semantic characteristics of verbal collocations $a_x^{VNonRef} a_y^{NObj} c_y^{Pac}$ of the predicate (5).

The next step, we obtain predicates of the semantic equivalence of two collocations for the substantive (represented by γ_{1L}), attributive (represented by γ_{2L}), verbal (represented by γ_{3L}) ones. For instance, the predicate of semantic equivalence of substantive collocations in Ukrainian and Russian corpora is defined as γ_{1U}:

$$\gamma_{1U}(x_1, y_1, x_2, y_2) = a_{x1}^{NNom} c_{y1}^{Ag} a_{y1}^{NGen} c_{y1}^{Att} \wedge a_{x2}^{NNom} c_{y2}^{Ag} a_{y2}^{NGen} c_{y2}^{Att} \tag{6}$$

We define the predicate of semantic equivalence of verbal collocations in English corpora as γ_{3E}:

$$\gamma_{3E}(x_1, y_1, x_2, y_2) = a_{x1}^{VNonRef} a_{y1}^{NObj} c_{y1}^{Pac} \wedge a_{x2}^{VNonRef} a_{y2}^{NObj} c_{y2}^{Pac} \tag{7}$$

We use thesauri to establish the synonymy between collocates. In the case of English, we utilize WordNet 3.1.0 of 151 806 unique nouns, verbs and adjectives, that contains synsets in every dictionary entry. For the Ukrainian language, we have developed a thesaurus of about 3 000 unique nouns, verbs and adjectives.

We assume that collocations can be considered as semantically similar if the main word x_1 of the collocation is synonymous with the main word x_2 in the second collocation as well as the dependent word y_1 is synonymous with y_2.

Therefore, collocations can be considered to be semantically close if (1) their grammatical and semantic features satisfy the predicate of equivalence and (2) the words of two collocations are synonymous in pairs. Table 1 shows the examples of three types of synonymous collocations extracted from our Ukrainian, Russian and English text corpora.

Table 1: The examples of three types of synonymous collocations extracted from Ukrainian, Russian and English text corpora

Collocations type	English language	Ukrainian, Russian languages
substantive (Noun-Noun)	health department – health officials	zastosuvannya komputera (the computer application) – vykorystannya noutbuka (the use of a laptop)
attributive (Adjective-Noun)	federal agents – federal investigators	suchasniy metod (the up-to-date method) – inovatsiyniy sposib (an innovative way)
verbal (Verb-Noun)	deliver assessments – present assessments	prepodnosit informatsiyu (to present the information) – predstavlat svedenia (to present the data)

4 Source data and experimental results

To evaluate the effectiveness of the proposed logical-linguistic model, we designed a corpus of more than 1 000 Ukrainian and Russian texts of scientific papers that contain more than 3,5 million words and about 2200 unique words. All papers are devoted to the broad theme of information technologies. As a result of the experiment, we extracted 62738 substantive, 46808 attributive and 3965 verbal semantically similar collocations. These collocations are similar in one or more pairs.

In order to evaluate our experimental results for the Ukrainian and Russian languages, we used experts' opinion. About 500 synonymous pairs of collocations were randomly extracted from the lists of these pairs for each language and presented for judgment. Three experts were asked to compare the similarity of meaning of the collocation pairs on the scale of from 0 to 2: 0 – the collocations don't have any semantic similarity, 2 – the pair of collocations has some semantic similarity, 1 – the experts find it difficult to answer. We considered the collocations in the pair as semantically similar when the average score of experts was more than 1.4. For example, when all the experts rated a pair of collocations as 2, the inter-rater agreement equaled to 2. If collocations were rated by two of experts as 2 and by one expert as 1, the inter-rater agreement equaled to 1.7. However, in cases of the inter-rater agreement of less than 1.4, the pair of collocations is thought as not semantically similar.

To evaluate the effectiveness of the model for extracting semantically similar collocations from the English corpus, we exploit Microsoft Research Paraphrase Corpus (MRPC), which consists of 5801 pairs of sentences obtained from thousands of news sources on the web. Fig 2 shows the example of the extraction of semantically similar collocations from two semantically similar sentences of the corpus.

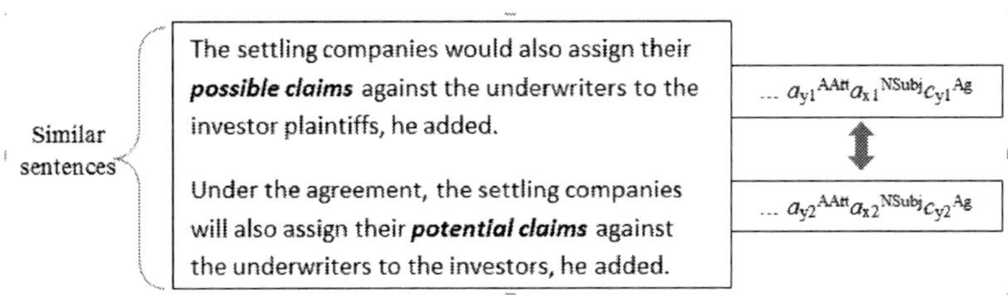

Figure 2: The example of the extraction of semantically similar collocations from two semantically similar sentences of MRPC corpus via the logical-linguistic equations

In MRPC all the pairs of sentences were rated by 2 judges as "semantically equivalent" or "non-equivalent". The inter-rater agreement was averaging 83% (Quirk et al., 2004).

As a result, precision, showing the correctness of the semantic similarity relation of collocations, is 0.7459 for Ukrainian and Russian texts and 0.8898 for English Microsoft Research Paraphrase Corpus. Relevant approaches extracted paraphrase fragment pairs with the precision of 67%, manually annotating fragment pairs as paraphrases, related or invalid (Wang and Callison-Burch, 2011) and 84%, rating fragment pairs as paraphrases, related or irrelevant with the inter-annotator agreement according to Cohen's Kappa of 0.67 (Regneri and Wang, 2012).

Additionally, using Microsoft Research Paraphrase Corpus we have been able to calculate the recall of the model. To do that we had hypothesized that whether sentences have a similar meaning they must contain similar collocations. Knowing the total amount of similar sentences in the corpus, we assume that each similar sentence pair contains one synonymous collocation pair. Consequently, to evaluate the recall of our experiments, we have computed the ratio between the number of semantically similar collocation pairs found (3650) to the total amount of sentence pairs specified as semantically equivalent (3900). Based on the hypothesis we calculated the recall of our model for English text as 94%.

5 Conclusions and Future Work

This paper proposes a novel logical-linguistic model for extraction of semantically similar two-word collocations from the Ukrainian, Russian and English corpora as an additional option of the first stage of generating the thesaurus automatically.

In order to assess our model, the corpora in various languages are exploited. We compute the precision of the model for Russian and Ukrainian languages on the basis of the corpus that comprises more than 1000 scientific articles devoted to the information technologies themes. To compute the precision of the model for English, we exploit MRPC. Additionally, since the corpus preliminary annotated we are able to calculate the recall of the model.

Our model achieves as a result over 74% precision of extraction of semantically similar collocations from Ukrainian and Russian corpora, about 89% from English one. Moreover, the recall of semantically similar collocations extraction from English Microsoft Research Paraphrase Corpus achieves over 94%. The task for further work is verification of our research results via probabilistic computation of occurrence of synonymous collocations in text corpora.

In future studies, we intend to broaden the scope of collocation types examination and to consider the combination of main parts of speech with auxiliary ones (e.g. prepositions, conjunctions etc.) that go beyond the scope of the model now. Additionally, in prospect, we intend to spread our dataset for free access to carry out similar approaches.

6 Acknowledgment

The research was funded in part by the Committee of Science of the Ministry of Education and Science of the Republic of Kazakhstan (project No. AP05131073 – Methods, models of retrieval and analyses of criminal contained information in semi-structured and unstructured textual arrays).

References

Akermi, I. and R. Faiz (2012). A novel method for word-pair similarity computing. *International Journal of Computational Linguistics Research 3*(4), 131–142.

Boom, C. D., S. V. Canneyt, S. Bohez, T. Demeester, and B. Dhoedt (2015). Learning semantic similarity for very short texts. *2015 ieee international conference on data mining workshop (icdmw)*, 1229–1234.

Dang, A., R. Makki, A. Moh'd, A. Islam, V. Keselj, and E. Milios (2016). Real time filtering of tweets using wikipedia concepts and google tri-gram semantic relatedness. *The Twenty-Fourth Text REtrieval Conference Proceedings* (2).

Ganitkevitch, J., B. V. Durme, and C. Callison-Burch (2013). Ppdb: The paraphrase database. *Proceedings of the 2013 Conference of the North American Chapter of the Association for Computational Linguistics: Human Language Technologies*, 758–764.

Han, L., T. Finin, P. McNamee, A. Joshi, and Y. Yesha (2013). Improving word similarity by augmenting pmi with estimates of word polysemy. *IEEE Transactions on Knowledge and Data Engineering 25*(6), 1307–1322.

Islam, A. and D. Inkpen (2006). Second order co-occurrence pmi for determining the semantic similarity of words. *LREC*, 1033–1038.

Islam, A. and D. Inkpen (2008). Semantic text similarity using corpus-based word similarity and string similarity. *ACM Transactions on Knowledge Discovery from Data (TKDD) 2*(2), 10:1–10:25.

Jarmasz, M. and S. Szpakowicz (2003). Thesaurus and semantic similarity. *Proceedings of the International Conference on Recent Advances in Natural Language Processing (RANLP-2003)*, 212–219.

Khairova, N., S. Petrasova, and P. S. Gautam, A. (2015). The logic and linguistic model for automatic extraction of collocation similarity. *Econtechmod an international quarterly journal 4*(4), 42–48.

Khairova, N., S. Petrasova, and P. S. Gautam, A. (2016). The logical-linguistic model of fact extraction from english texts. *International Conference on Information and Software Technologies*, 625–635.

McCrae, J. P., K. Asooja, N. Aggarwal, and P. Buitelaar (2016). Nuig-unlp at semeval-2016 task 1: Soft alignment and deep learning for semantic textual similarity. *Proceedings of the 10th International Workshop on Semantic Evaluation (SemEval-2016)*, 712–717.

Pavlick, E., J. Bos, M. Nissim, C. Beller, B. V. Durme, and C. Callison-Burch (2015). Adding semantics to data-driven paraphrasing. *roc. of ACL-IJCNLP. Beijing, China.*

Pedersen, T., S. Pakhomov, S. Patwardhan, and G. Chute, C. (2007). Measures of semantic similarity and relatedness in the biomedical domain. *Journal of biomedical informatics 40*(3), 288–299.

Pirró, G. and N. Seco (2008). Design, implementation and evaluation of a new semantic similarity metric combining features and intrinsic information content. *OTM Confederated International Conferences" On the Move to Meaningful Internet Systems"*, 1271–1288.

Quirk, C., C. Brockett, and W. B. Dolan (2004). Monolingual machine translation for paraphrase generation. *In Proceedings of the 2004 Conference on Empirical Methods in Natural Language Processing*, 142–149.

Rakib, M. R. H., A. Islam, and E. Milios (2016). f: Phrase relatedness function using overlapping bi-gram context. *Canadian Conference on Artificial Intelligence*, 137–149.

Regneri, M. and R. Wang (2012). Using discourse information for paraphrase extraction. *Proceedings of the 2012 Joint Conference on Empirical Methods in Natural Language Processing and Computational Natural Language Learning*, 916–927.

Sultan, M. A., S. Bethard, and T. Sumner (2014). Back to basics for monolingual alignment: Exploiting word similarity and contextual evidence. *Transactions of the Association for Computational Linguistics 2*, 219–230.

Sultan, M. A., S. Bethard, and T. Sumner (2015). Dls@ cu: Sentence similarity from word alignment and semantic vector composition. *SemEval*, 148–153.

Wang, R. and C. Callison-Burch (2011). Paraphrase fragment extraction from monolingual comparable corpora. *Proceedings of the 4th Workshop on Building and Using Comparable Corpora: Comparable Corpora and the Web*, 525–60.

Detecting Paraphrases of Standard Clause Titles in Insurance Contracts

Frieda Josi
University of Applied Sciences and Arts
Hanover
frieda.josi@hs-hannover.de

Christian Wartena
University of Applied Sciences and Arts
Hanover
christian.wartena@hs-hannover.de

Ulrich Heid
University of Hildesheim
Institute for Information Science
and Natural Language Processing
heid@uni-hildesheim.de

Abstract

For the analysis of contract texts, validated model texts, such as model clauses, can be used to identify used contract clauses. This paper investigates how the similarity between titles of model clauses and headings extracted from contracts can be computed, and which similarity measure is most suitable for this. For the calculation of the similarities between title pairs we tested various variants of string similarity and token based similarity. We also compare two additional semantic similarity measures based on word embeddings using pre-trained embeddings and word embeddings trained on contract texts. The identification of the model clause title can be used as a starting point for the mapping of clauses found in contracts to verified clauses.

1 Introduction

The calculation of text similarities is a key factor in the analysis of texts that consist of recurring text parts or that have to correspond to formulation patterns. In the insurance industry, there is a multitude of individual contracts between companies and insurance companies, or between insurance companies and reinsurance companies. However, most contracts more or less standardized clauses and text templates. In order to find the structure of a contract and to support the contract review, it is important to find all parts in the contract that are based on standardized clauses.

In our work, we compare a heading in the contract to be analyzed with all clause titles in a collection of model clauses. We have two reasons to do this title-based comparison: in the first place we work with scanned PDF texts. Thus we have to reconstruct the often complicated layout structure of the contract text. For the extraction of text we apply *pdfminer*, a Python PDF parser [1]. We use a trained classifier to identify headers, footers, enumeration elements, headings, stamps and hand-written remarks. We describe our procedure of layout-based structure recognition and analysis in Josi and Wartena (2018). Once we can identify titles of model clauses, we know what type of formatting is used for clause titles, and we can split up the main part of the contract text into a list of clause text blocks. Second, comparing the text of the clause bodies with all possible candidate model clauses requires less effort, if our system identifies the model clause candidate(s) based on their titles. An overview of the work presented here and its place in the overall project workflow is given in Figure 1. The subject of this paper concerns the first point from Figure 1, the similarity calculation of the model clauses.

In some cases, the title found in a contract is identical to the title of a model clause. In many cases, however the titles differ. We can identify many patterns of variation, such as addition or omission of

[1] PDFMiner: `https://pypi.org/project/pdfminer/`

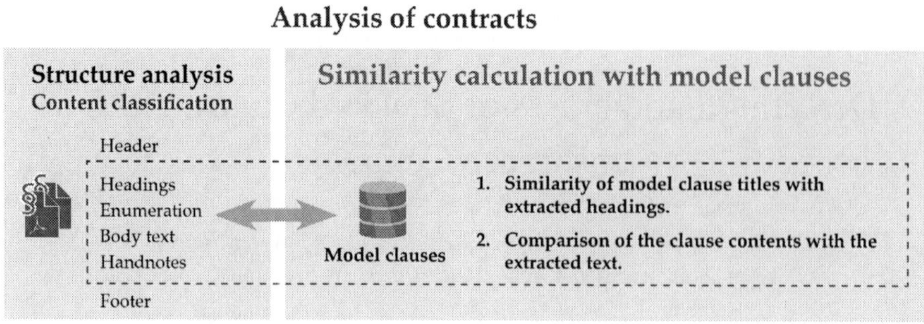

Figure 1: Overview of contract analysis with the section of similarity calculation of model clauses

Table 1: Titles of extracted clauses and their corresponding model clauses.

Extracted title	Model clause title	Change
ULTIMATE NET LOSS CLAUSE	Ultimate Net Loss	Extension
CONTRACT CONTINUITY CLAUSE (LSW 1035)	Contract Continuity Clause - Retro	Refinement
Choice of Law And Jurisdiction:	Governing Law and Jurisdiction	Lexical substitution
Arbitration ARIAS (UK) 1997 (G231.n:-	Arias Arbitration Clause	Refinement
Condition 15 ERRORS AND OMISSIONS	Errors and Omissions	Extension listing

the word *Clause*, addition of a colon at the end, a number in the beginning, etc. Some examples of such variations are given in Table 1. In addition, we have OCR errors and errors in the extraction of the headings, especially when the headings consist of several lines and are placed in the left margin, which is quite normal for insurance contracts.

If we manually defined a number of patterns of allowed variations, we would risk overfitting on the clauses we have seen and missing many unseen variations. Instead, we would like to use a simple similarity measure to compare the clause titles. The rest of the paper deals with the selection of the best similarity measure for this task. In order to evaluate similarity measures we constructed two sets of clause titles. The first set contains pairs of corresponding and non-corresponding titles. The task here is to predict whether two titles correspond or not. The second set contains a large number of extracted headings from contracts. The task is to predict which headings correspond to the title of a model clause.

2 Related Work

The calculation of text similarity is used in many applications and projects and is constantly extended and improved. To calculate similarities between very short text pairs and to match the correct titles of the model clauses with the extracted headings, we have used state-of-the-art methods and measurement approaches which we have adapted for our application and trained with our data set of contract texts. The particular problem we faced is that the text pairs are very short. On average, the titles consist of 24 characters and not a single title has more than nine words.

Bär et al. (2012) define a semantic textual similarity with character and word n-grams by a semantic vector comparison and a word similarity comparison based on lexical-semantic sources is performed using various similarity features. The authors apply a logarithmic-linear regression model and use *Explicit Semantic Analysis*, a vector based representation of text for semantic similarity measurements, to replace nouns. Further evaluations of similarity measurements of longer sentences are described by Achananuparp et al. (2008). Their evaluation measures are based on semantic equivalence, when the sentence pairs do not have the same surface shape. Whereby: sentences are similar, when they are paraphrases of each other, contain the same subject, or when one sentence is the super set of the other.

In (Bhagat and Hovy, 2013) similarities of paraphrases are defined and analyzed in terms of e.g. synonym substitution or part substitution. In total they describe 25 possible substitution types. Some of these types are also contained in our dataset of clause titles and model clause titles. Kovatchev et al. (2018) compare texts with different lengths on the similarity of their meaning. They attach much importance to detailed error analysis and have built a corpus in which paraphrases and negations are annotated. For the text pairs, the similarity is measured by paraphrase deductions in both texts. Another approach focusing on the analysis of paraphrases is described by Benikova and Zesch (2017). In this paper, different granulation levels of paraphrase sentences and annotated verb argument structures of paraphrases are compared for the similarity calculation. They distinguish between event paraphrase, lexical paraphrase, wording and inverse lexical paraphrase. In (Agirre et al., 2012) the semantic equivalence of two texts with paraphrase differences is measured. This is achieved by using common tokens in the sentence. For the vectors of the sentences the cosine similarity is calculated. The text pairs in their work consist of 51 words up to 126 words. Gomaa and Fahmy (2013) suggest to combine several similarity metrics to determine string-based, corpus-based, and knowledge-based similarities. For the string based approach they use the *Longest Common Sub String (LCS) algorithm* and various editing distance metrics like *Jaro*, *Damerau-Levenshtein* and *N-grams*. For the term-based similarity measurement *Manhattan Distance*, *Cosine similarity* and *Jaccard Distance*. Also Aldarmaki and Diab (2018) evaluate combined models for similarity measurement and evaluate the results of a logistic regression classifier by calculating the cosine similarity between two sentence vectors. Lan and Xu (2018) compare and evaluate seven LSTM-based methods for sentence pair modeling on eight commonly used datasets, such as Quora (Question Pairs Dataset), Twitter URL Corpus, and PIT-2015 (Paraphrase and Semantic Similarity in Twitter). For small datasets, they propose the method *Pairwise Word Interaction Model* (introduced in (He and Lin, 2016)).

Boom et al. (2015) recommend a combined method of word embedding and tf.idf weighting to calculate the similarity of text fragments (20 words per fragment). In this method, text parts with terms of a high tf.idf weighting are used. Kenter and de Rijke (2015) present a text similarity calculation, where they use the similarity of word vectors to derive semantic meta features, which in turn are used for training a supervised classifier. Kusner et al. (2015) present a distance measurement between text documents based on word embeddings and the dissimilarity of two probability distributions over words. *Word Mover's Distance* calculates the minimum vector distance of words from one document to words from another document.

3 Chosen Similarity Measures

To determine the optimal similarity calculation of text pairs we use character-based and token-based measurement methods. As can be seen in Table 1, the text fragments of our text pairs are very short, sometimes a single title consists of only one word. The longest title has nine words in total, the shortest title consists of a total of 5 characters. Hence, we compare the similarity measurement methods on character and token basis.

In addition, we determine the similarity of the title pairs with the support of word embeddings. We use the Word Mover's Distance measurement (Kusner et al., 2015), which combines word overlap with word similarities, thus considering substitution of words by semantically similar words. As another measurement, we have calculated the cosine distance of the average values of the word vectors to obtain an optimal threshold for separating the prediction of whether a title pair matches. For both methods using word embeddings we have used embeddings trained on a corpus of reinsurance contracts as well as embeddings from the pre-trained GoogleNews model[2].

3.1 Trigram Overlap

For the character-based similarity of the title pairs, we use the Jaccard coefficient of the set of all character trigrams that can be extracted from the titles. We do not use special symbols for the beginning and the end

[2]Used pre-trained model: GoogleNews-vectors-negative300.bin

of the string. This causes a slightly lower influence of changes at the beginning and the end of the string. We use N-grams based on the methodology of Markov (1913) and Shannon (1948) and the calculation of the Jaccard coefficient as described by Jaccard (1901).

3.2 Edit Distance

The edit distance between two strings is defined as the minimum number of edit operations necessary to change one string into the other one. We then use the edit distance to determine the number of edits in relation to the length of the strings. If $d(s,t)$ is the edit distance between titles s and t, we used $sim_d = 1 - \frac{d(s,t)}{\max(|s|,|t|)}$. Thus the value of sim_d is 0 if no alignment is possible and 1 if s and t are identical. We calculate the distance between the title pairs based on the minimal edit distance (Levenshtein, 1966).

3.3 Weighted Edit Distance

The weighted edit distance makes use of includes the following penalties: for substitution, insertion and deletion we use a penalty of 0.1 if a non-alphabetic character is involved, and a penalty of 1.0 otherwise.

3.4 Word Overlap

To predict the best threshold between equivalent and non-equivalent title pairs based on their tokens, we calculate the word overlap with the Jaccard coefficient, as we did for the trigram overlap in Section 3.1. We include only words in the comparison and completely disregard differences in punctuation in all token based methods. Since titles consist of only few words and they often are not completely identical, we also test a variant using stemming. We used the Lancaster Stemmer (Paice, 1990) because it reduces the words to a very short stem allowing to match different words with the same root. The results are clearly better than those obtained using lemmatization only. In Table 2 some examples of stemmed title pairs are shown.

Table 2: Comparison of some examples of tokenized title pairs reduced with Lancaster stemming for word overlap calculation

Tokenized title pairs	Tokenized title pairs + Lancaster stemming
[reinstatement clause] [reinstatements]	[**reinst** claus] [**reinst**]
[reinstatement provisions] [reinstatements]	[**reinst** provid] [**reinst**]
[reinstatement] [reinstatements]	**[reinst] [reinst]**
[terrorism **exclusion** clause] [terror war **exclusion**]	[**ter exclud** claus] [**ter** war **exclud**]

3.5 Vector Space Model

For the cosine similarity we again use stemmed titles. We experiment with two different vector weights: term frequency and tf.idf. We compute the idf weights on the set of all extracted headings and all titles of model clauses. Consequently, words like *clause* get a low weight.

3.6 Average Word Embeddings

We use two similarity measures in which the words are represented by word embeddings. These methods should be able to detect the similarity of two sentences in which a word is replaced by a synonym. As a first approach we represent a title by the average of all word embeddings of the words in the sentence. We use the cosine distance to compare the representations of two titles. We use these averaged word embeddings both with pre-trained embeddings and with embeddings trained on texts from the insurance domain.

In order to train domain-specific word embeddings, we used a collection of 3,730 insurance contracts with 15,831,789 lemmatized words after removing stop words and punctuation. We first use our developed layout-based structural analysis method to separate the contents of the contracts from the text elements in the headers and footers. For training word vectors we use the text from contract content. In addition, we use the text of the model clauses and some other full texts from contracts.

The texts of the insurance contracts that we use for training our model are pre-processed. We use the tokenization and sentence splitting of the Natural Language Toolkit (nltk)[3]. All texts are lemmatized by the TreeTagger (Schmid, 1994). Finally, we remove all stop words (stop word list from nltk). The Open-Source Toolkit gensim[4] is used for vector modelling. We train vectors with 150 dimensions and used a window size of 3.

3.7 Word Mover's Distance

Word Mover's Distance (WMD) is a measure that compares two probability distributions of words and is defined as the minimum effort that is needed to move the probabilities from words in the starting distribution to words in the other distribution. The effort is defined as the sum of the probabilities moving from each word to another word multiplied with their distance, where the distance between two words is defined as the Euclidian distance between the word embeddings of the words. In order to obtain a similarity measure between 0 and 1 based on the WMD, we define $sim_{\text{WMD}}(s,t) = \frac{1}{1+\text{WMD}(s,t)}$.

As weights for the word distribution we use again pure term frequency and tf.idf weighting, and again we test the method with Google News Word embeddings and with our own word embeddings.

4 Experimental Setup

In the first experiment we evaluate the various distance measures on a classification task in which equivalent pairs of titles have to be distinguished from non-equivalent pairs of titles. The second experiment is a retrieval experiment in which all titles corresponding to the title of a model clause have to be found in a set of all headings extracted from a number of contracts.

4.1 Classification of Equivalent and Non-Equivalent Title Pairs

To calculate the similarity, we use 309 model clauses provided by the insurance company. We use a small subset (3730 contracts) of a large number of available contracts for the development of analysis methods. The methods are successively tested on a more comprehensive set of contracts. For the selection of a similarity measure we took six contracts, extracted all headings and manually selected all model clauses used in these contracts. This resulted in a set of 103 pairs where the model titles and our headings match (our gold standard), and we built a negative test set with an incorrect assignment to a model clause title (103 negative title pairs).

To find the threshold that marks the separation between positive and a negative pairs, for each above mentioned similarity measure, we compute the accuracy with varying thresholds.

4.2 Retrieval of Model Clause Titles from a Set of Extracted Title Candidates

We analyzed six contracts and extracted all clauses with their headings from all clause text sections and manually annotated for each clause whether it corresponds to a model clause or not. The data set consists of 494 extracted headings for which a match is to be found in the data set of 154 model clause titles. The goal for the task at hand is to have an automatic method deciding for each heading, whether it is the heading of a clause corresponding to a model case or not. We can either define this as a binary classification problem or as a retrieval problem where we have to find all model clause headings from the set of all headings.

We use a kind of nearest-neighbor approach to solve the task: if the similarity of a title with some model clause title exceeds a defined threshold, we classify it as a model clause title. The goal of this

[3]Natural Language Toolkit: `https://www.nltk.org`

[4]Gensim library: `https://radimrehurek.com/gensim`

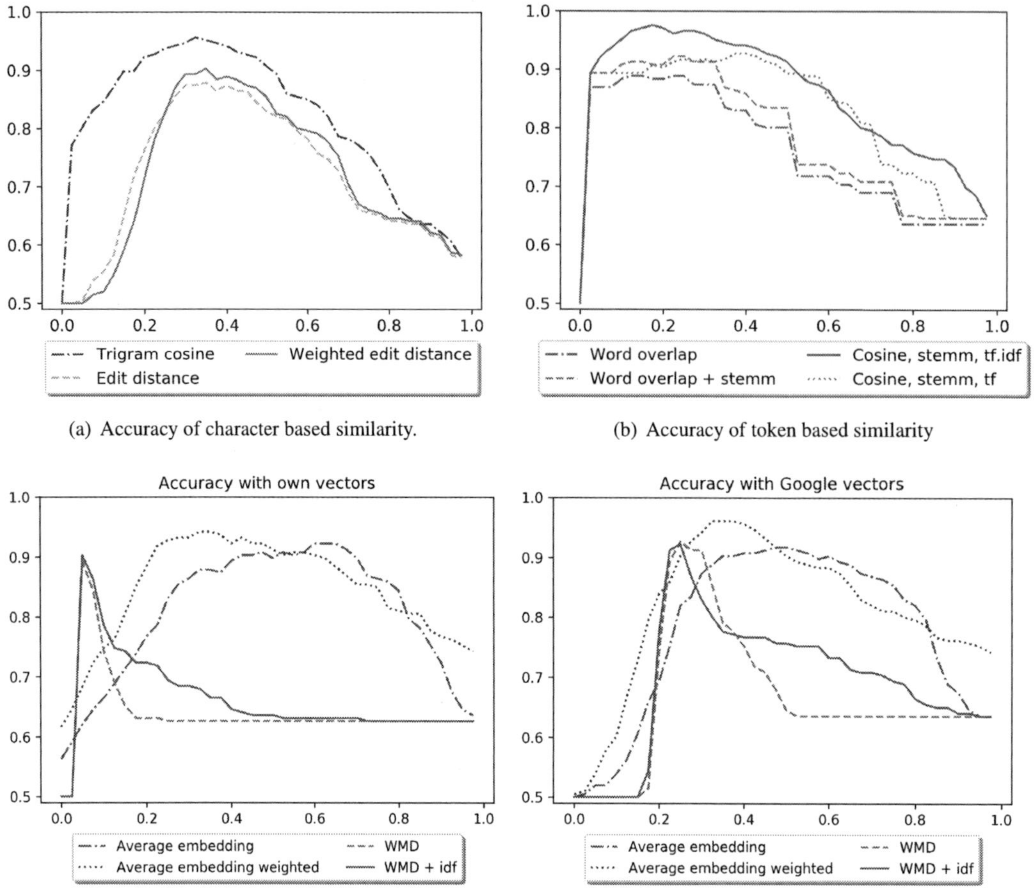

(a) Accuracy of character based similarity.

(b) Accuracy of token based similarity

(c) Accuracy of our word2vec model

(d) Accuracy of pre-trained word2vec model

Figure 2: Accuracy of matching title pairs (Accuracy (y), Threshold (x)).

experiment is to find the subset of extracted titles which match the titles of model clauses. The similarity to the most similar model clause title gives a natural way to rank the result. We evaluate this ranking with the typical evaluation measures for rankings: average precision and area under the ROC curve (AUC). We also determine the maximum achievable accuracy and the corresponding optimal threshold to split the ranking into relevant and non-relevant results.

5 Results

The results of the first experiment (described in Section 4.1) are summarized in Table 3 and Figure 3. Here we identify the threshold for which we achieved the highest accuracy. This describes the similarity of the corresponding title pairs for the similarity measurement method we used. Table 5 shows examples and their prediction values for incorrectly predicted title pairs from the first experiment.

In Table 5, for the title pair [BIOLOGICAL OR CHEMICAL MATERIALS EXCLUSION][Genetically Modified Organism Exclusion Clause - Exclusion] only the measurement method *Cosine of weighted average word embedding* with pre-trained vectors of Google made a correct prediction (with 0.42). The pair contains different words that are semantically related. This kind of paraphrase is only captured when the word embeddings are used. However, in other cases these methods find a similarity where the titles do not correspond: In the case of the title pair [Class of Business:][Service of Suit] both methods using Google's

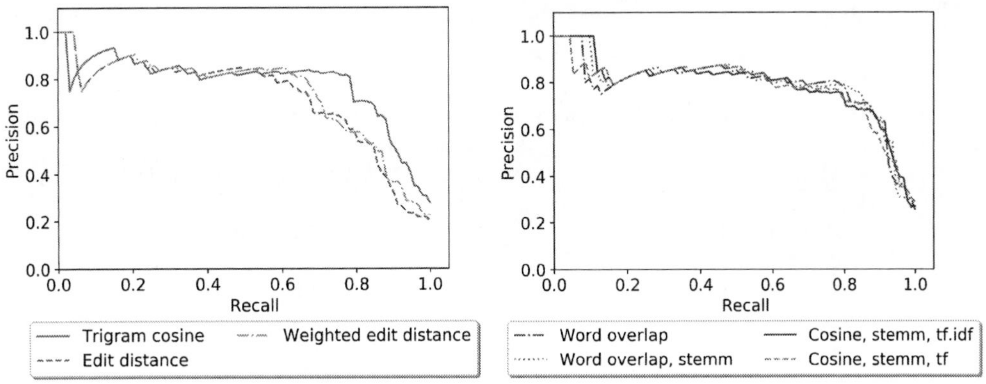

(a) String based methods

(b) Token based methods

Figure 3: Evaluate retrieval on decision of being a template heading

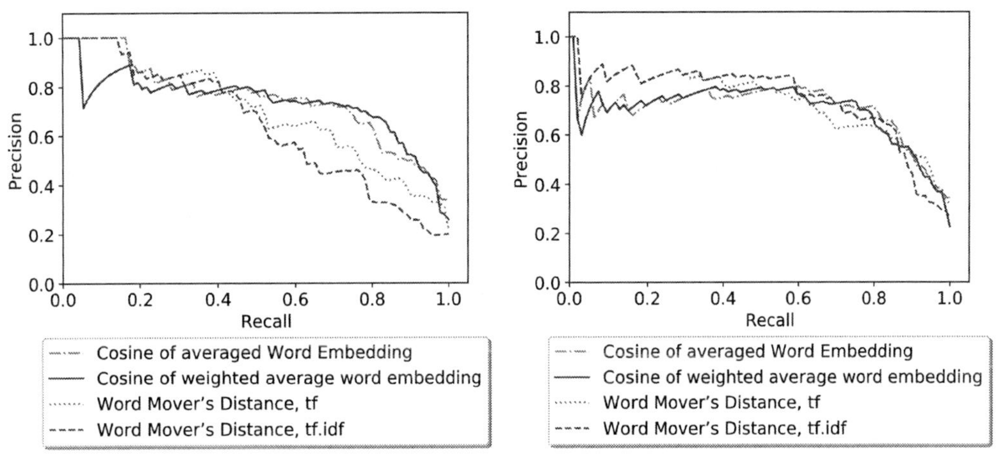

(a) Own Word Embeddings

(b) Google News Word Embeddings

Figure 4: Evaluate retrieval on decision of being a template heading, with Word Embeddings

pre-trained vectors made an incorrect decision. For title pairs like [Inspection of Records Clause][Access to Records] or [Choice of Law][Governing Law and Jurisdiction] the measurement methods with the pre-trained vectors and also the weighted cosine distance calculation made a correct prediction. The calculation of trigrams and word overlap give false negatives here.

The second experiment is described in Section 4.2. Table 4 and Figure 3 and 4 show the results for the methods that were used. Here we evaluated whether an extracted contract title corresponds to a model clause title. We show the threshold value we get for the highest accuracy. Then we calculate the average precision (AP) and the area under the curve (AUC).

6 Conclusion

The vector space model using cosine, stemming and tf.idf weights has achieved an accuracy of 0.98 in the classification task (experiment 1) and 0.91 in the retrieval task (experiment 2) and thus seems best suited to continue our work on contract analysis. The high accuracy of this method can be explained by the use of aggressive stemming, enabling the match of singular and plural forms of a word and by the use of idf weighting, which minimizes the influence of words like *clause, condition, retro* that are often added or

Table 3: Experiment 1: Classification of title pairs into corresponding vs. non-corresponding ones - max. accuracy

Method	Max accuracy	(Threshold)
String based		
Trigram cosine	0.96	(0.33)
Edit distance	0.88	(0.35)
Weighted edit distance	0.90	(0.35)
Token based		
Word overlap	0.89	(0.13)
Word overlap, stemming	0.92	(0.23)
Cosine, stemming, tf.idf	**0.98**	(0.18)
Cosine, stemming, tf	0.93	(0.38)
Custom Word Embeddings		
Cosine of averaged word embedding	0.92	(0.60)
Cosine of weighted average word embedding	0.94	(0.33)
Word Mover's Distance, tf	0.89	(0.05)
Word Mover's Distance, tf.idf	0.90	(0.05)
Google News Word Embeddings		
Cosine of averaged word embedding	0.92	(0.48)
Cosine of weighted average word embedding	0.96	(0.33)
Word Mover's Distance, tf	0.93	(0.25)
Word Mover's Distance, tf.idf	0.92	(0.25)

Table 4: Results for Retrieval-Evaluation (Experiment 2). Average precision (AP), Area under the curve (AUC)

Method	AP	AUC	Max Accuracy	(Threshold)
String based				
Trigram cosine	0.79	0.76	0.93	(0.60)
Edit distance	0.73	0.71	0.90	(0.59)
Weighted edit distance	0.74	0.73	0.91	(0.64)
Token based				
Word overlap	0.80	0.76	0.93	(0.40)
Word overlap, stemming	0.80	0.76	0.93	(0.40)
Cosine, stemming tf.idf	0.79	0.76	0.91	(0.60)
Cosine, stemming tf	0.79	0.76	0.92	(0.61)
Custom Word Embeddings				
Average word embedding	0.75	0.75	0.90	(0.80)
Cosine of weighted average word embedding	0.74	0.75	0.90	(0.68)
Word Mover's Distance, tf	0.70	0.72	0.88	(0.14)
Word Mover's Distance, tf.idf	0.64	0.67	0.87	(0.27)
Google News Word Embeddings				
Cosine of averaged word embedding	0.73	0.76	0.90	(0.76)
Cosine of weighted average word embedding	0.73	0.75	0.90	(0.66)
Word Mover's Distance, tf	0.76	0.76	0.89	(0.39)
Word Mover's Distance, tf.idf	0.77	0.75	0.90	(0.43)

Table 5: Incorrectly classified title pairs from experiment 1. Cells contain the computed similarity. In case the computed similarity leads to wrong classification (using the optimal threshold as given in the second line of the table), the cell has a red background.

Title pair	Real	Trigram cosine	Word overlap, stemm.	Cosine, stemm., tf.idf	Google WMD, tf.idf	Google wgt. av. w2v
Threshold		0.60	0.23	0.18	0.25	0.33
Inspection of Records Clause / Access to Records	+	0.30	0.17	0.34	0.28	0.43
Choice of Law / Governing Law and Jurisdiction	+	0.11	0.17	0.31	0.26	0.43
NOTICE OF LOSS / Loss Settlements	+	0.15	0.25	0.28	0.22	0.17
Exclusions: / Exclusions (general) - Exclusions	+	0.78	0.33	0.49	0.27	0.33
Simultaneous Settlements Clause / Loss Settlements	+	0.55	0.25	0.46	0.23	0.27
BIOLOGICAL OR CHEMICAL MATERIALS EXCLUSION / Genetically Modified Organism Exclusion Clause - Exclusion	+	0.36	0.1	0.07	0.22	0.42
CURRENCY CLAUSE / Currency Conversion	+	0.54	0.33	0.62	0.29	0.72
INTERMEDIARY CLAUSE / Period Clause	-	0.37	0.33	0.16	0.21	0.07
Class of Business: / Service of Suit	-	0.14	0.2	0.07	0.25	0.33
TAXES / Federal Excise Tax Clause	-	0.12	0.25	0.44	0.25	0.66
ULTIMATE NET LOSS / Loss Settlements	-	0.14	0.25	0.24	0.23	0.23

removed from the standard title. Somewhat surprisingly, the WMD method does not give an equally good result. We attribute this to the fact that the exchange of synonyms rarely occurs in the title pairs. Thus, we also do not expect better results from other approaches using word embeddings.

Summarizing the result, we can conclude that there are no large differences between the different measures. In almost all cases, idf-weighting (using document frequency in headings) improves the results. Also, all methods using word embeddings yielded better results with the pre-trained Google News word embeddings than with the embeddings trained on our contract corpus.

Returning to our analysis of scanned PDF files: we need to find a significant number of model clause titles to find out what type of formatting is used for clause titles. Once we have detected the formatting of clause titles in a contract we can split up the contract into clauses, sub-clauses and so on and compare the full text of each clause with the model clause text. Experiment 2 shows that we can retrieve about half of the model clause titles with a precision of over 0.8 (see Figure 4). Interestingly, this high precision combined with 50% recall is only reached by the Word Mover's Distance with tf.idf values.

Acknowledgments

This research was financed by *Hannover Rück SE*. We would like to thank Dr. Julia Perl for many useful comments and *Hannover Rück SE* for making available the contracts.

References

Achananuparp, P., X. Hu, and X. Shen (2008). The Evaluation of Sentence Similarity Measures. In I.-Y. Song, J. Eder, and T. M. Nguyen (Eds.), *Data Warehousing and Knowledge Discovery*, Volume 5182, pp. 305–316. Berlin, Heidelberg: Springer Berlin Heidelberg.

Agirre, E., D. Cer, M. Diab, and A. Gonzalez-Agirre (2012). SemEval-2012 Task 6: A Pilot on Semantic Textual Similarity.

Aldarmaki, H. and M. Diab (2018). Evaluation of Unsupervised Compositional Representations.

Benikova, D. and T. Zesch (2017, November). Same same, but different: Compositionality of Paraphrase Granularity Levels. In *RANLP 2017 - Recent Advances in Natural Language Processing Meet Deep Learning*, pp. 90–96. Incoma Ltd. Shoumen, Bulgaria.

Bhagat, R. and E. Hovy (2013, September). What Is a Paraphrase? *Computational Linguistics 39*(3), 463–472.

Boom, C. D., S. V. Canneyt, S. Bohez, T. Demeester, and B. Dhoedt (2015, November). Learning Semantic Similarity for Very Short Texts. In *2015 IEEE International Conference on Data Mining Workshop (ICDMW)*, pp. 1229–1234.

Bär, D., C. Biemann, I. Gurevych, and T. Zesch (2012). UKP: Computing Semantic Textual Similarity by Combining Multiple Content Similarity Measures.

Gomaa, W. H. and A. A. Fahmy (2013, April). A Survey of Text Similarity Approaches. *International Journal of Computer Applications 68*(13), 13–18.

He, H. and J. J. Lin (2016). Pairwise Word Interaction Modeling with Deep Neural Networks for Semantic Similarity Measurement. In *HLT-NAACL*, pp. 937–948.

Jaccard, P. (1901). Étude comparative de la distribution florale dans une portion des Alpes et des Jura. *Bulletin del la Société Vaudoise des Sciences Naturelles 37*, 547–579.

Josi, F. and C. Wartena (2018). Structural Analysis of Contract Renewals. In *Proceedings of the ACM CIKM 2018 Workshops*, Turin.

Kenter, T. and M. de Rijke (2015). Short Text Similarity with Word Embeddings. In *Proceedings of the 24th ACM International Conference on Information and Knowledge Management*, CIKM '15, New York, NY, USA, pp. 1411–1420. ACM. event-place: Melbourne, Australia.

Kovatchev, V., M. A. Marti, and M. Salamo (2018). ETPC - A Paraphrase Identification Corpus Annotated with Extended Paraphrase Typology and Negation.

Kusner, M. J., Y. Sun, N. I. Kolkin, and K. Q. Weinberger (2015). From Word Embeddings to Document Distances. In *Proceedings of the 32d International Conference on Machine Learning - Volume 37*, ICML'15, pp. 957–966. JMLR.org. event-place: Lille, France.

Lan, W. and W. Xu (2018). Neural Network Models for Paraphrase Identification, Semantic Textual Similarity, Natural Language Inference, and Question Answering. arXiv: 1806.04330.

Levenshtein, V. I. (1966). Binary Codes Capable of Correcting Deletions, Insertions and Reversals. *Soviet Physics Doklady 10.*

Markov, A. A. (1913). Essai d'une recherche statistique sur le texte du roman "Eugene Onegin" illustrant la liaison des epreuve en chain ('Example of a statistical investigation of the text of "Eugene Onegin" illustrating the dependence between samples in chain') | BibSonomy. pp. 153–162.

Paice, C. D. (1990). Another Stemmer. *SIGIR Forum 24*(3), 56–61.

Schmid, H. (1994). Probabilistic Part-of-Speech Tagging Using Decision Trees. In *International Conference on New Methods in Language Processing*, Manchester, UK, pp. 44–49.

Shannon, C. E. (1948). A Mathematical Theory of Communication. *Bell System Technical Journal 27*(3), 379–423.

Semantic Matching of Documents from Heterogeneous Collections: A Simple and Transparent Method for Practical Applications

Mark-Christoph Müller
Heidelberg Institute for Theoretical Studies gGmbH
Heidelberg, Germany
mark-christoph.mueller@h-its.org

Abstract

We present a very simple, unsupervised method for the pairwise matching of documents from heterogeneous collections. We demonstrate our method with the Concept-Project matching task, which is a binary classification task involving pairs of documents from heterogeneous collections. Although our method only employs standard resources without any domain- or task-specific modifications, it clearly outperforms the more complex system of the original authors. In addition, our method is *transparent*, because it provides explicit information about how a similarity score was computed, and *efficient*, because it is based on the aggregation of (pre-computable) word-level similarities.

1 Introduction

We present a simple and efficient unsupervised method for pairwise matching of documents from *heterogeneous* collections. Following Gong et al. (2018), we consider two document collections heterogeneous if their documents differ systematically with respect to vocabulary and / or level of abstraction. With these *defining* differences, there often also comes a difference in length, which, however, by itself does not make document collections heterogeneous. Examples include collections in which *expert* answers are mapped to *non-expert* questions (e.g. *InsuranceQA* by Feng et al. (2015)), but also so-called *community* QA collections (Blooma and Kurian (2011)), where the lexical mismatch between Q and A documents is often less pronounced than the length difference.

Like many other approaches, the proposed method is based on word embeddings as universal meaning representations, and on vector cosine as the similarity metric. However, instead of computing pairs of document representations and measuring their similarity, our method assesses the document-pair similarity on the basis of selected pairwise word similarities. This has the following advantages, which make our method a viable candidate for practical, real-world applications: **efficiency**, because pairwise word similarities can be efficiently (pre-)computed and cached, and **transparency**, because the selected words from each document are available as evidence for what the similarity computation was based on.

We demonstrate our method with the *Concept-Project matching* task (Gong et al. (2018)), which is described in the next section.

2 Task, Data Set, and Original Approach

The *Concept-Project matching* task is a binary classification task where each instance is a pair of heterogeneous documents: one **concept**, which is a short science curriculum item from NGSS[1], and one **project**, which is a much longer science project description for school children from ScienceBuddies[2].

[1] https://www.nextgenscience.org

[2] https://www.sciencebuddies.org

CONCEPT LABEL: ecosystems: - ls2.a: interdependent relationships in ecosystems
CONCEPT DESCRIPTION: Ecosystems have carrying capacities , which are limits to the numbers of organisms and populations they can support . These limits result from such factors as the availability of living and nonliving resources and from such challenges such as predation , competition , and disease . Organisms would have the capacity to produce populations of great size were it not for the fact that environments and resources are finite . This fundamental tension affects the abundance (number of individuals) of species in any given ecosystem .

PROJECT LABEL: Primary Productivity and Plankton
PROJECT DESCRIPTION: Have you seen plankton? I am not talking about the evil villain trying to steal the Krabby Patty recipe from Mr. Krab. I am talking about plankton that live in the ocean. In this experiment you can learn how to collect your own plankton samples and see the wonderful diversity in shape and form of planktonic organisms. The oceans contain both the earth's largest and smallest organisms. Interestingly they share a delicate relationship linked together by what they eat. The largest of the ocean's inhabitants, the Blue Whale, eats very small plankton, which themselves eat even smaller phytoplankton. All of the linkages between predators, grazers, and primary producers in the ocean make up an enormously complicated food web.The base of this food web depends upon phytoplankton, very small photosynthetic organisms which can make their own energy by using energy from the sun. These phytoplankton provide the primary source of the essential nutrients that cycle through our ocean's many food webs. This is called primary productivity, and it is a very good way of measuring the health and abundance of our fisheries.There are many different kinds of phytoplankton in our oceans. [...] One way to study plankton is to collect the plankton using a plankton net to collect samples of macroscopic and microscopic plankton organisms. The net is cast out into the water or trolled behind a boat for a given distance then retrieved. Upon retrieving the net, the contents of the collecting bottle can be removed and the captured plankton can be observed with a microscope. The plankton net will collect both phytoplankton (photosynthetic plankton) and zooplankton (non-photosynthetic plankton and larvae) for observation.In this experiment you will make your own plankton net and use it to collect samples of plankton from different marine or aquatic locations in your local area. You can observe both the abundance (total number of organisms) and diversity (number of different kinds of organisms) of planktonic forms to make conclusions about the productivity and health of each location. In this experiment you will make a plankton net to collect samples of plankton from different locations as an indicator of primary productivity. You can also count the number of phytoplankton (which appear green or brown) compared to zooplankton (which are mostly marine larval forms) and compare. Do the numbers balance, or is there more of one type than the other? What effect do you think this has on productivity cycles? Food chains are very complex. Find out what types of predators and grazers you have in your area. You can find this information from a field guide or from your local Department of Fish and Game. Can you use this information to construct a food web for your local area? Some blooms of phytoplankton can be harmful and create an anoxic environment that can suffocate the ecosystem and leave a "Dead Zone" behind. Did you find an excess of brown algae or diatoms? These can be indicators of a harmful algal bloom. Re-visit this location over several weeks to report on an increase or decrease of these types of phytoplankton. Do you think that a harmful algal bloom could be forming in your area? For an experiment that studies the relationship between water quality and algal bloom events, see the Science Buddies project Harmful Algal Blooms in the Chesapeake Bay.

Figure 1: C-P Pair (Instance 261 of the original data set.)

The publicly available data set[3] contains 510 labelled pairs[4] involving $C = 75$ unique concepts and $P = 230$ unique projects. A pair is annotated as 1 if the project matches the concept (57%), and as 0 otherwise (43%). The annotation was done by undergrad engineering students. Gong et al. (2018) do not provide any specification, or annotation guidelines, of the semantics of the 'matches' relation to be annotated. Instead, they create gold standard annotations based on a majority vote of three manual annotations. Figure 1 provides an example of a matching C-P pair. The concept labels can be very specific, potentially introducing vocabulary that is not present in the actual concept descriptions. The extent to which this information is used by Gong et al. (2018) is not entirely clear, so we experiment with several setups (cf. Section 4).

2.1 Gong et al. (2018)'s Approach

The approach by Gong et al. (2018) is based on the idea that the longer document in the pair is reduced to a set of *topics* which capture the essence of the document in a way that eliminates the effect of a potential length difference. In order to overcome the vocabulary mismatch, these topics are not based on *words* and their distributions (as in LSI (Deerwester et al. (1990)) or LDA (Blei et al. (2003))), but on word embedding vectors. Then, basically, matching is done by measuring the cosine similarity between the topic vectors and the short document words. Gong et al. (2018) motivate their approach mainly with the length mismatch argument, which they claim makes approaches relying on document representations (incl. vector averaging) unsuitable. Accordingly, they use Doc2Vec (Le and Mikolov (2014)) as one of their baselines, and show that its performance is inferior to their method. They do not, however, provide a much simpler averaging-based baseline. As a second baseline, they use Word Mover's Distance (Kusner et al. (2015)), which is based on word-level distances, rather than distance of global document representations, but which also fails to be competitive with their topic-based method. Gong et al. (2018) use two different sets of word embeddings: One (topic_wiki) was trained on a full English Wikipedia dump, the other (wiki_science) on a smaller subset of the former dump which only contained science articles.

3 Our Method

We develop our method as a simple alternative to that of Gong et al. (2018). We aim at comparable or better classification performance, but with a simpler model. Also, we design the method in such a way that it provides human-interpretable results in an efficient way. One common way to compute

[3] `https://github.com/HongyuGong/Document-Similarity-via-Hidden-Topics`
[4] Of the original 537 labelled pairs, 27 were duplicates, which we removed.

the similarity of two documents (i.e. word sequences) c and p is to average over the word embeddings for each sequence first, and to compute the cosine similarity between the two averages afterwards. In the first step, weighting can be applied by multiplying a vector with the TF, IDF, or TF*IDF score of its pertaining word. We implement this standard measure (**AVG_COS_SIM**) as a baseline for both our method and for the method by Gong et al. (2018). It yields a single scalar similarity score. The core idea of our alternative method is to turn the above process upside down, by computing the cosine similarity of *selected* pairs of words from c and p first, and to average over the similarity scores afterwards (cf. also Section 6). More precisely, we implement a measure **TOP_n_COS_SIM_AVG** as the average of the n highest pairwise cosine similarities of the n top-ranking words in c and p. Ranking, again, is done by TF, IDF, and TF*IDF. For each ranking, we take the top-ranking n words from c and p, compute $n \times n$ similarities, rank by decreasing similarity, and average over the top n similarities. This measure yields both a scalar similarity score and a list of $< c_x, p_y, sim >$ tuples, which represent the qualitative aspects of c and p on which the similarity score is based.

4 Experiments

Setup All experiments are based on off-the-shelf word-level resources: We employ WOMBAT (Müller and Strube (2018)) for easy access to the 840B GloVe (Pennington et al. (2014)) and the GoogleNews[5] Word2Vec (Mikolov et al. (2013)) embeddings. These embedding resources, while slightly outdated, are still widely used. However, they cannot handle out-of-vocabulary tokens due to their fixed, word-level lexicon. Therefore, we also use a pretrained English fastText model[6] (Bojanowski et al. (2017); Grave et al. (2018)), which also includes subword information. IDF weights for approx. 12 mio. different words were obtained from the English Wikipedia dump provided by the Polyglot project (Al-Rfou et al. (2013)). All resources are case-sensitive, i.e. they might contain different entries for words that only differ in case (cf. Section 5).

We run experiments in different setups, varying both the input representation (GloVe vs. Google vs. fastText embeddings, $\pm$ TF-weighting, and $\pm$ IDF-weighting) for concepts and projects, and the extent to which concept descriptions are used: For the latter, **Label** means only the concept *label* (first and second row in the example), **Description** means only the textual *description* of the concept, and **Both** means the concatenation of **Label** and **Description**. For the projects, we always use both label and description. For the project descriptions, we extract only the last column of the original file (CONTENT), and remove user comments and some boiler-plate. Each instance in the resulting data set is a tuple of $< c, p, label >$, where c and p are bags of words, with case preserved and function words[7] removed, and $label$ is either 0 or 1.

Parameter Tuning Our method is unsupervised, but we need to define a threshold parameter which controls the *minimum* similarity that a concept and a project description should have in order to be considered a match. Also, the TOP_n_COS_SIM_AVG measure has a parameter n which controls how many ranked words are used from c and p, and how many similarity scores are averaged to create the final score. Parameter tuning experiments were performed on a random subset of 20% of our data set (54% positive). Note that Gong et al. (2018) used only 10% of their 537 instances data set as tuning data. The tuning data results of the best-performing parameter values for each setup can be found in Tables 1 and 2. The top F scores per type of concept input (Label, Description, Both) are given in **bold**. For AVG_COS_SIM and TOP_n_COS_SIM_AVG, we determined the threshold values (T) on the tuning data by doing a simple .005 step search over the range from 0.3 to 1.0. For TOP_n_COS_SIM_AVG, we additionally varied the value of n in steps of 2 from 2 to 30.

[5]`https://code.google.com/archive/p/word2vec/`

[6]`https://dl.fbaipublicfiles.com/fasttext/vectors-crawl/cc.en.300.bin.gz`

[7]We use the list provided by Gong et al. (2018), with an additional entry for *cannot*.

Results The top **tuning data** scores for AVG_COS_SIM (Table 1) show that the Google embeddings with TF*IDF weighting yield the top F score for all three concept input types (.881 - .945). Somewhat expectedly, the best overall F score (.945) is produced in the setting **Both**, which provides the most information. Actually, this is true for all four weighting schemes for both GloVe and Google, while fastText consistently yields its top F scores (.840 - .911) in the **Label** setting, which provides the least information. Generally, the level of performance of the simple baseline measure AVG_COS_SIM on this data set is rather striking.

Concept Input →			Label				Description				Both			
Embeddings	**TF**	**IDF**	**T**	**P**	**R**	**F**	**T**	**P**	**R**	**F**	**T**	**P**	**R**	**F**
GloVe	-	-	.635	.750	.818	.783	.720	.754	.891	.817	.735	.765	.945	.846
	+	-	.640	.891	.745	.812	.700	.831	.891	.860	.690	.813	.945	.874
	-	+	.600	.738	.873	.800	.670	.746	.909	.820	.755	.865	.818	.841
	+	+	.605	.904	.855	.879	.665	.857	.873	.865	.715	.923	.873	.897
Google	-	-	.440	.813	.945	.874	.515	.701	.982	.818	.635	.920	.836	.876
	+	-	.445	.943	.909	**.926**	.540	.873	.873	.873	.565	.927	.927	.927
	-	+	.435	.839	.945	.889	.520	.732	.945	.825	.590	.877	.909	.893
	+	+	.430	.943	.909	**.926**	.530	.889	.873	**.881**	.545	.945	.945	**.945**
fastText	-	-	.440	.781	.909	.840	.555	.708	.927	.803	.615	.778	.891	.831
	+	-	.435	.850	.927	.887	.520	.781	.909	.840	.530	.803	.964	.876
	-	+	.435	.850	.927	.887	.525	.722	.945	.819	.600	.820	.909	.862
	+	+	.420	.895	.927	.911	.505	.803	.891	.845	.520	.833	.909	.870

Table 1: Tuning Data Results **AVG_COS_SIM**. Top F per Concept Input Type in **Bold**.

For TOP_n_COS_SIM_AVG, the **tuning data** results (Table 2) are somewhat more varied: First, there is no single best performing set of embeddings: Google yields the best F score for the **Label** setting (.953), while GloVe (though only barely) leads in the **Description** setting (.912). This time, it is fastText which produces the best F score in the **Both** setting, which is also the best overall **tuning data** F score for TOP_n_COS_SIM_AVG (.954). While the difference to the Google result for **Label** is only minimal, it is striking that the best overall score is again produced using the 'richest' setting, i.e. the one involving both TF and IDF weighting and the most informative input.

Concept Input →			Label				Description				Both			
Embeddings	**TF**	**IDF**	**T/n**	**P**	**R**	**F**	**T/n**	**P**	**R**	**F**	**T/n**	**P**	**R**	**F**
GloVe	+	-	.365/6	.797	.927	.857	.690/14	.915	.782	.843	.675/16	.836	.927	.879
	-	+	.300/30	.929	.236	.377	.300/30	.806	.455	.581	.300/30	.778	.636	.700
	+	+	.330/6	.879	.927	.903	.345/6	.881	.945	**.912**	.345/6	.895	.927	.911
Google	+	-	.345/22	.981	.927	**.953**	.480/16	.895	.927	.911	.520/16	.912	.945	.929
	-	+	.300/30	1.00	.345	.514	.300/8	1.00	.345	.514	.300/30	1.00	.600	.750
	+	+	.300/10	1.00	.509	.675	.300/14	.972	.636	.769	.350/22	1.00	.836	.911
fastText	+	-	.415/22	.980	.873	.923	.525/14	.887	.855	.870	.535/20	.869	.964	.914
	-	+	.350/24	1.00	.309	.472	.300/30	1.00	.382	.553	.300/28	1.00	.673	.804
	+	+	.300/20	1.00	.800	.889	.300/10	.953	.745	.837	.310/14	.963	.945	**.954**

Table 2: Tuning Data Results **TOP_n_COS_SIM_AVG**. Top F per Concept Input Type in **Bold**.

We then selected the best performing parameter settings for every concept input and ran experiments on the held-out **test data**. Since the original data split used by Gong et al. (2018) is unknown, we cannot exactly replicate their settings, but we also perform ten runs using randomly selected 10% of our 408 instances test data set, and report average P, R, F, and standard deviation. The results can be found in Table 3. For comparison, the two top rows provide the best results of Gong et al. (2018).

The first interesting finding is that the AVG_COS_SIM measure again performs very well: In all three settings, it beats both the system based on general-purpose embeddings (topic_wiki) and the one that is adapted to the science domain (topic_science), with again the **Both** setting yielding the best overall result (.926). Note that our **Both** setting is probably the one most similar to the concept input used by Gong et al. (2018). This result corroborates our findings on the tuning data, and clearly contradicts the (implicit) claim made by Gong et al. (2018) regarding the infeasibility of document-level matching for documents of different lengths. The second, more important finding is that our proposed TOP_n_COS_SIM_AVG measure is also very competitive, as it also outperforms both systems by Gong et al. (2018) in two out of

						P		R		F	
Gong et al. (2018)	topic_science					.758	±.012	.885	±.071	.818	±.028
	topic_wiki					.750	±.009	.842	±.010	.791	±.007
Method	**Embeddings**	**Settings**		**T/n**	**Conc. Input**						
AVG_COS_SIM	Google	+TF	+IDF	.515	Label	.939	±.043	.839	±.067	.884	±.038
	Google	+TF	+IDF	.520	Description	.870	±.068	.834	±.048	.849	±.038
	Google	+TF	+IDF	.545	Both	.915	±.040	.938	±.047	**.926**	±.038
TOP_n_COS_SIM_AVG	Google	+TF	-IDF	.345/22	Label	.854	±.077	.861	±.044	.856	±.054
	GloVe	+TF	+IDF	.345/6	Description	.799	±.063	.766	±.094	.780	±.068
	fastText	+TF	+IDF	.310/14	Both	.850	±.059	.918	±.049	**.881**	±.037

Table 3: Test Data Results

three settings. It only fails in the setting using only the **Description** input.[8] This is the more important as we exclusively employ off-the-shelf, general-purpose embeddings, while Gong et al. (2018) reach their best results with a much more sophisticated system and with embeddings that were custom-trained for the science domain. Thus, while the performance of our proposed TOP_n_COS_SIM_AVG method is superior to the approach by Gong et al. (2018), it is itself outperformed by the 'baseline' AVG_COS_SIM method with appropriate weighting. However, apart from raw classification performance, our method also aims at providing human-interpretable information on how a classification was done. In the next section, we perform a detail analysis on a selected setup.

5 Detail Analysis

The similarity-labelled word pairs from concept and project description which are selected during classification with the TOP_n_COS_ SIM_AVG measure provide a way to qualitatively evaluate the basis on which each similarity score was computed. We see this as an advantage over average-based comparison (like AVG_COS_SIM), since it provides a means to check the plausibility of the decision. Here, we are mainly interested in the overall best result, so we perform a detail analysis on the best-performing **Both** setting only (fastText, TF*IDF weighting, $T = .310$, $n = 14$). Since the *Concept-Project matching* task is a binary classification task, its performance can be qualitatively analysed by providing examples for instances that were classified correctly (True Positive (TP) and True Negative (TN)) or incorrectly (False Positive (FP) and False Negative (FN)).
Table 5 shows the concept and project words from selected instances (one TP, FP, TN, and FN case each) of the tuning data set. Concept and project words are ordered alphabetically, with concept words appearing more than once being grouped together. According to the selected setting, the number of word pairs is $n = 14$. The bottom line in each column provides the average similarity score as computed by the TOP_n_COS_SIM_AVG measure. This value is compared against the threshold $T = .310$. The similarity is higher than T in the TP and FP cases, and lower otherwise. Without going into too much detail, it can be seen that the selected words provide a reasonable idea of the gist of the two documents. Another observation relates to the effect of using unstemmed, case-sensitive documents as input: the top-ranking words often contain inflectional variants (e.g. *enzyme* and *enzymes*, *level* and *levels* in the example), and words differing in case only can also be found. Currently, these are treated as distinct (though semantically similar) words, mainly out of compatibility with the pretrained GloVe and Google embeddings. However, since our method puts a lot of emphasis on individual words, in particular those coming from the shorter of the two documents (the *concept*), results might be improved by somehow merging these words (and their respective embedding vectors) (see Section 7).

6 Related Work

While in this paper we apply our method to the *Concept-Project matching* task only, the underlying task of matching text sequences to each other is much more general. Many existing approaches follow

[8]Remember that this setup was only minimally superior (.001 F score) to the next best one on the tuning data.

TP (**.447** > .310)			FP (**.367** > .310)			TN (**.195** < .310)			FN (**.278** < .310)		
Concept Word	**Project Word**	**Sim**	**Concept Word**	**Project Word**	**Sim**	**Concept Word**	**Project Word**	**Sim**	**Concept Word**	**Project Word**	**Sim**
cells	enzymes	.438	co-evolution	dynamic	.299	energy	allergy	.147	area	water	.277
cells	genes	.427	continual	dynamic	.296	energy	juice	.296	climate	water	.269
molecules	DNA	.394	delicate	detail	.306	energy	leavening	.186	earth	copper	.254
molecules	enzyme	.445	delicate	dynamic	.326	energy	substitutes	.177	earth	metal	.277
molecules	enzymes	.533	delicate	texture	.379	surface	average	.212	earth	metals	.349
molecules	gene	.369	dynamic	dynamic	1.00	surface	baking	.216	earth	water	.326
molecules	genes	.471	dynamic	image	.259	surface	egg	.178	extent	concentration	.266
multiple	different	.550	dynamic	range	.377	surface	leavening	.158	range	concentration	.255
organisms	enzyme	.385	dynamic	texture	.310	surface	thickening	.246	range	ppm	.237
organisms	enzymes	.512	surface	level	.323	transfer	baking	.174	systems	metals	.243
organisms	genes	.495	surface	texture	.383	transfer	substitute	.192	systems	solution	.275
organs	enzymes	.372	surface	tiles	.321	transfer	substitutes	.157	typical	heavy	.299
tissues	enzymes	.448	systems	dynamic	.272	warms	baking	.176	weather	heavy	.248
tissues	genes	.414	systems	levels	.286	warms	thickening	.214	weather	water	.308
	Avg. Sim	**.447**		Avg. Sim	**.367**		Avg. Sim	**.195**		Avg. Sim	**.278**

Table 4: **TOP_n_COS_SIM_AVG** Detail Results of Best-performing fastText Model on **Both**.

the so-called *compare-aggregate* framework (Wang and Jiang (2017)). As the name suggests, these approaches collect the results of element-wise matchings (*comparisons*) first, and create the final result by aggregating these results later. Our method can be seen as a variant of *compare-aggregate* which is characterized by extremely simple methods for comparison (cosine vector similarity) and aggregation (averaging). Other approaches, like He and Lin (2016) and Wang and Jiang (2017), employ much more elaborated supervised neural networks methods. Also, on a simpler level, the idea of averaging similarity scores (rather than scoring averaged representations) is not new: Camacho-Collados and Navigli (2016) use the average of pairwise word similarities to compute their *compactness score*.

7 Conclusion and Future Work

We presented a simple method for semantic matching of documents from heterogeneous collections as a solution to the *Concept-Project matching* task by Gong et al. (2018). Although much simpler, our method clearly outperformed the original system in most input settings. Another result is that, contrary to the claim made by Gong et al. (2018), the standard averaging approach does indeed work very well even for heterogeneous document collections, if appropriate weighting is applied. Due to its simplicity, we believe that our method can also be applied to other text matching tasks, including more 'standard' ones which do not necessarily involve **heterogeneous** document collections. This seems desirable because our method offers additional transparency by providing not only a similarity score, but also the subset of words on which the similarity score is based. Future work includes detailed error analysis, and exploration of methods to combine complementary information about (grammatically or orthographically) related words from word embedding resources. Also, we are currently experimenting with a pretrained ELMo (Peters et al. (2018)) model as another word embedding resource. ELMo takes word embeddings a step further by dynamically creating *contextualized* vectors from input word sequences (normally sentences). Our initial experiments have been promising, but since ELMo tends to yield *different*, context-dependent vectors for the *same* word in the *same* document, ways have still to be found to combine them into single, document-wide vectors, without (fully) sacrificing their context-awareness.
The code used in this paper is available at `https://github.com/nlpAThits/TopNCosSimAvg`.

Acknowledgements The research described in this paper was funded by the Klaus Tschira Foundation. We thank the anonymous reviewers for their useful comments and suggestions.

References

Al-Rfou, R., B. Perozzi, and S. Skiena (2013, August). Polyglot: Distributed word representations for multilingual nlp. In *Proceedings of the Seventeenth Conference on Computational Natural Language Learning*, Sofia, Bulgaria, pp. 183–192. Association for Computational Linguistics.

Blei, D. M., A. Y. Ng, and M. I. Jordan (2003). Latent dirichlet allocation. *Journal of Machine Learning Research 3*, 993–1022.

Blooma, M. J. and J. C. Kurian (2011). Research issues in community based question answering. In P. B. Seddon and S. Gregor (Eds.), *Pacific Asia Conference on Information Systems, PACIS 2011: Quality Research in Pacific Asia, Brisbane, Queensland, Australia, 7-11 July 2011*, pp. 29. Queensland University of Technology.

Bojanowski, P., E. Grave, A. Joulin, and T. Mikolov (2017). Enriching word vectors with subword information. *TACL 5*, 135–146.

Camacho-Collados, J. and R. Navigli (2016). Find the word that does not belong: A framework for an intrinsic evaluation of word vector representations. In *Proceedings of the 1st Workshop on Evaluating Vector-Space Representations for NLP, RepEval@ACL 2016, Berlin, Germany, August 2016*, pp. 43–50. Association for Computational Linguistics.

Deerwester, S. C., S. T. Dumais, T. K. Landauer, G. W. Furnas, and R. A. Harshman (1990). Indexing by latent semantic analysis. *JASIS 41*(6), 391–407.

Feng, M., B. Xiang, M. R. Glass, L. Wang, and B. Zhou (2015). Applying deep learning to answer selection: A study and an open task. In *2015 IEEE Workshop on Automatic Speech Recognition and Understanding, ASRU 2015, Scottsdale, AZ, USA, December 13-17, 2015*, pp. 813–820. IEEE.

Gong, H., T. Sakakini, S. Bhat, and J. Xiong (2018). Document similarity for texts of varying lengths via hidden topics. In *Proceedings of the 56th Annual Meeting of the Association for Computational Linguistics (Volume 1: Long Papers)*, pp. 2341–2351. Association for Computational Linguistics.

Grave, E., P. Bojanowski, P. Gupta, A. Joulin, and T. Mikolov (2018). Learning word vectors for 157 languages. In N. Calzolari, K. Choukri, C. Cieri, T. Declerck, S. Goggi, K. Hasida, H. Isahara, B. Maegaard, J. Mariani, H. Mazo, A. Moreno, J. Odijk, S. Piperidis, and T. Tokunaga (Eds.), *Proceedings of the Eleventh International Conference on Language Resources and Evaluation, LREC 2018, Miyazaki, Japan, May 7-12, 2018*. European Language Resources Association (ELRA).

He, H. and J. J. Lin (2016). Pairwise word interaction modeling with deep neural networks for semantic similarity measurement. In K. Knight, A. Nenkova, and O. Rambow (Eds.), *NAACL HLT 2016, The 2016 Conference of the North American Chapter of the Association for Computational Linguistics: Human Language Technologies, San Diego California, USA, June 12-17, 2016*, pp. 937–948. The Association for Computational Linguistics.

Kusner, M. J., Y. Sun, N. I. Kolkin, and K. Q. Weinberger (2015). From word embeddings to document distances. In F. R. Bach and D. M. Blei (Eds.), *Proceedings of the 32nd International Conference on Machine Learning, ICML 2015, Lille, France, 6-11 July 2015*, Volume 37 of *JMLR Workshop and Conference Proceedings*, pp. 957–966. JMLR.org.

Le, Q. V. and T. Mikolov (2014). Distributed representations of sentences and documents. In *Proceedings of the 31th International Conference on Machine Learning, ICML 2014, Beijing, China, 21-26 June 2014*, Volume 32 of *JMLR Workshop and Conference Proceedings*, pp. 1188–1196. JMLR.org.

Mikolov, T., I. Sutskever, K. Chen, G. S. Corrado, and J. Dean (2013). Distributed representations of words and phrases and their compositionality. In *Proceedings of Advances in Neural Information Processing Systems 26*. Lake Tahoe, Nev., 5–8 December 2013, pp. 3111–3119.

Müller, M. and M. Strube (2018). Transparent, efficient, and robust word embedding access with WOMBAT. In D. Zhao (Ed.), *COLING 2018, The 27th International Conference on Computational Linguistics: System Demonstrations, Santa Fe, New Mexico, August 20-26, 2018*, pp. 53–57. Association for Computational Linguistics.

Pennington, J., R. Socher, and C. D. Manning (2014). Glove: Global vectors for word representation. In A. Moschitti, B. Pang, and W. Daelemans (Eds.), *Proceedings of the 2014 Conference on Empirical Methods in Natural Language Processing, EMNLP 2014, October 25-29, 2014, Doha, Qatar, A meeting of SIGDAT, a Special Interest Group of the ACL*, pp. 1532–1543. ACL.

Peters, M. E., M. Neumann, M. Iyyer, M. Gardner, C. Clark, K. Lee, and L. Zettlemoyer (2018). Deep contextualized word representations. In M. A. Walker, H. Ji, and A. Stent (Eds.), *Proceedings of the 2018 Conference of the North American Chapter of the Association for Computational Linguistics: Human Language Technologies, NAACL-HLT 2018, New Orleans, Louisiana, USA, June 1-6, 2018, Volume 1 (Long Papers)*, pp. 2227–2237. Association for Computational Linguistics.

Wang, S. and J. Jiang (2017). A compare-aggregate model for matching text sequences. In *5th International Conference on Learning Representations, ICLR 2017, Toulon, France, April 24-26, 2017, Conference Track Proceedings*. OpenReview.net.

Association for Computational Linguistics
209 N. Eighth Street
Stroudsburg, Pennsylvania 18360

ISBN 978-1-5108-8764-0

CURRAN ASSOCIATES INC.
proceedings.com